'The laws of Man on Earth are not made for the individual but for the majority . . .'

In *Candlelight* T. Lobsang-Rampa uses his best endeavours to explain the laws and the consequences of obeying or disregarding them. Dr. Rampa considers all life on earth to be a school and every living creature to be a pupil of that school; the disobedient ones will take longer to graduate than the pupils who want to learn and willingly accept knowledge, their reward is ascension to a higher grade where there are new things to learn and fewer hardships to overcome. The path to knowledge and happiness may be through the darkest of nights, but a little *Candlelight* will make the going easier . . .

Also by Dr T. Lobsang-Rampa

THE THIRTEENTH CANDLE
THE HERMIT
FEEDING THE FLAME
LIVING WITH THE LAMA
BEYOND THE TENTH
CHAPTERS OF LIFE (*Illustrated*)
THE SAFFRON ROBE
YOU—FOREVER
THE RAMPA STORY
WISDOM OF THE ANCIENTS
DOCTOR FROM LHASA
THE THIRD EYE
THE CAVE OF THE ANCIENTS

and published by Corgi Books

Dr. T. Lobsang-Rampa

Candlelight

CORGI BOOKS
A DIVISION OF TRANSWORLD PUBLISHERS LTD
A NATIONAL GENERAL COMPANY

CANDLELIGHT
A CORGI BOOK 0 552 09390 4

First publication in Great Britain

PRINTING HISTORY
Corgi edition published 1973

Copyright © T. Lobsang-Rampa 1973

This book is set in Plantin 10/10½ pt.

Corgi Books are published by Transworld Publishers, Ltd.,
Cavendish House, 57–59 Uxbridge Road, Ealing, London W.5

Made and printed in Great Britain by
Richard Clay (The Chaucer Press), Ltd., Bungay, Suffolk.

**NOTE: The Australian price appearing on the
back cover is the recommended retail price.**

To
Kathleen Murata,
who has passed through
the Flames of Hardship –
and emerged Purified.

CANDLELIGHT

The faint flickering gleam of fourteen little Candles shines forth into the world, bringing to a vast number of people some of the Light of astral knowledge.

The Sunlight is waning. Coming fast is the end of Day. The Darkness of communism is by stealth and treachery engulfing the world faster and faster.

Soon the Light of Freedom will be extinguished for a time while Mankind ponders opportunities lost, and regrets warnings unheeded.

But even in the darkest hour there shall be the gleams of little Candles, bringing hope to a stricken world. The darkest hour is before the dawn, and that hour is not yet.

The gloom and despondency of evil men usurping power shall be lessened by the knowledge that all suffering shall eventually pass, and the Sunlight shall shine again.

Candlelight may bring illumination to some, hope to others. Sunlight gives way to darkness, darkness gives way to Sunlight, but even in the deepest dark a Candle may show the Way.

FROM AN ADMIRER

'You are old, Father Rampa,' the Young Man exclaimed,
  'And the Press for too long have you defamed.
The Candles you lit gleam both near and afar
  Sending out light like a welcoming Star.'

'You are old, Father Rampa,' the Young Man said.
  'Put aside your typing, it's time that you died.
Your life has been hard and your experiences grim,
  But the Candles you lit will *never* grow dim!'

'You are old, Father Rampa,' the Young Man said.
  'Your Candles will flame long after you're dead.
The Truths you have taught will enrich our way,
  The hardships you suffered; *was* it too much to pay?'

Freed from suffering, freed from sorrow,
  Freed from worries about 'tomorrow',
Freed from the toils of this bad Earth,
  Freed from the circle of 'endless' re-birth,
Your life-flame flickers and ends one day,
  But the Candles *you* lit will show *us* the Way!

(with apologies to all and everyone who merits an apology!)

9

CHAPTER ONE

The sullen clouds came lowering out of the steel sky and began to weep. A thin veil of pattering raindrops scudded across the dirty roofs of Montreal and ended up as rivulets of sooty-black in the garbage-cluttered gutters. The tempo of the downpour increased; the swirling rainstorm blotted out the bridges, the tall, ugly buildings, and then even the Port itself.

Suddenly the trees leaned over, water pouring from depressed leaves, forming scummy puddles over the sparse grass. In the distance a ship hooted forlornly as though in despair at having again to enter Montreal, the City of Two Tongues.

Glumly the cats sat before the fogged-up window and wondered if the sun would ever shine again. Outside on the flooded roadway, a tattered copy of a French-language newspaper blew to its rightful home in a sewer where it momentarily blocked the water flow and then vanished in a scurry of gurgling sound.

The old blue bus went chuntering along, engine roaring, wheels flinging plumes of water from the flooded road. Came a CRASH as it dropped into the hollow by the office. Lurching and reeling, it pushed its cumbersome way through the murk and turned right, out of sound. There came the ponderous roar of the garbage truck pounding its way along the road. A behemoth shape glimpsed dimly through the unlighted gloom and then—Peace, save for the drumming of the rain.

The old man in the wheelchair groped for the light switch as he turned away from the steamed window. With the light on he turned sadly to the pile of letters yet to be answered. 'Questions—questions—questions,' he mumbled, 'do they think I

11

am a free advisory bureau on everything from conception to death—with a good dose of the hereafter thrown in?'

The letter from the 'lady' in a large U.S.A. city was interesting: 'I have read all thirteen of your books,' she wrote. 'A *good* author would have told all that and more in one-half chapter.' Gee, Ma'am, well—*thanks*! But—here they come: a very *very* cross Women's Lib gangster from Winnipeg. Doesn't like me a bit—thinks I *hate* women. Well, *she* is not a woman, anyhow, more like a drunken buck navvy from her language. Women? I *love* 'em. Men, and women, just the opposite sides of 'the coin'. Why *should* I hate them? What a *touchy* lot some women are, though, phooey!

But the minute minority do not matter. Most—about ninety-nine per cent (true) are sincerely interested in what I write and just 'love' my Candles. They want to know more about all aspects of metaphysics. How to levitate, how to teleport, how to do *this* and how to do *that*.

Quite a number of people have become increasingly interested in dowsing and pendulums. There is a letter here from a person who saw a man walking across a field, and suddenly the forked stick which the man was holding twitched violently. The correspondent tells me that this person was a water diviner, and please would I say if there is anything in this business of dowsing and using a pendulum.

Yes, most definitely dowsing is a genuine thing—if one knows how to use the hazel or other forked twig. Most definitely there is something in pendulums provided the person knows what he is or she is doing and is not just putting on a stage turn to impress the unwary.

First, we have to know what causes these things to work. At the present time with radio commonplace it is not at all difficult to get over the idea that there are certain currents, or certain waves, which a person cannot detect without some intermediary. For example, about us all the time is a horrible commotion which, fortunately, we cannot hear, but radio waves are coming in from everywhere—AM, FM, Long Waves, Short Waves, High Frequency, and Ultra-High Frequency. To the average human they might just as well not be there because without special apparatus or special conditions one just cannot perceive them. But—let us get a mysterious piece of equipment between the incoming waves and the loud-speaker or the television tube, and then we get noise or we get pictures. The mysterious piece of apparatus is connected usually to some substance (the aerial) which receives the incoming waves and then takes them to the interior of the mysterious box where all sorts of wires, bits of copper and mica or paper, etc., sort out the jumble and 'detect' a coherent signal. Then it passes on to another section of the box where it is amplified and its speed of frequency is reduced to that which can be dealt with. From the amplifier it goes to the output stage, and thence on to the speaker or to a television tube and speaker, and then we get something which approximates more or less to the original noise which was broadcast, or to the original picture which was broadcast. Of course, that is over-simplifying rather dreadfully because in addition to having the incoming signals we have to have a method of collecting the signals, detecting the signals, amplifying them, and putting them to 'output'. But—and we must not forget this—we have to have a method of tuning to the frequency or wavelength to which we desire to listen or watch.

Radio and dowsing are very much the same.

The signals we receive in dowsing—let's forget all about dowsing, shall we? Actually, unless a person is going to dowse for water only out in the 'blue yonder' there is no point in having hazel twigs, aluminium 'twigs', or all sorts of wonderful glorified versions of hazel twigs. It is much better and much more convenient to use a pendulum which does everything a dowsing rod can do, and much more. So let us just refer to pendulums because, unless you are a farmer in the wildest part of Australia where you can perhaps cut a suitable twig at any moment, there is no point in cluttering yourself with a lot of lumber.

A pendulum is a lump of material attached to something which will not constrict its movements. A little later we will discuss different types of pendulums, but basically the radiations which can be indicated by a pendulum are radiations in some way similar to radio. They are radiations transmitted by all and every material as it decomposes, or gets ready to change

13

state. We know, for example, that throughout countless years radium decays into lead. We know that all matter is a whole horde of molecules hopping about like fleas on a hot plate, the smaller the fleas the faster they can jump, the bigger the fleas the slower and more cumbersome. So it is with material. Everything has its atomic number, number of atoms indicating how slowly it is going to vibrate, or how fast it is going to vibrate. So all we do in pendulum work is to tune in to some atomic vibrations, and, if we know how, we can tell which one it is and where it is.

When we are dealing with radio we have an aerial system which absorbs or attracts or intercepts (call it what you like) the waves coming through the atmosphere. Perhaps they are bounced back by the Heaviside layer or the Appleton layer. But in addition there is a ground wire which makes contact with the ground wave because you must have two—positive and negative—in everything. You can take the ground wave as negative and the air wave as positive. So in the matter of pendulums the human body collects the air wave, acting as the antenna or aerial, and the feet in contact with the ground act as the earth connection, or 'ground'. And for correct pendulum work it is necessary to keep the balls of the feet on the ground unless one uses another method of tapping the earth current.

Of course, using a pendulum is simplicity itself. It is even simpler than simplicity if we know *why* a thing works. That is why you are getting this long collection of words which might at first strike you as rigmarole; it's not. Until you know what you are doing you can't tell when you are doing it!

Pendulums really work! Many Japanese tell the sex of unborn babies by the use of a pendulum. They use a gold ring suspended on a piece of string or thread, and it is held above the stomach of the pregnant woman. The direction or type of movement indicates the sex of the child yet to be born. Incidentally, many Chinese and Japanese use a pendulum for sexing eggs!

A radio set uses electric current for reproducing sound which was broadcast from some distant station. Television sets use current also for reproducing a rough simulacrum of the picture transmitted from a distant station. So in the same way if we are going to dowse or use a pendulum or anything else we have first of all to have a source of current, and the best source of current we can use is the human body. After all, our brains are really storage batteries, telephone exchanges, and all that sort of thing, but the main thing is, it is a source of electric current sufficient for all our needs and sufficient to enable us to 'detect' impulses and thereby cause a pendulum to twitch, swirl, gyrate, or oscillate, or all the other queer thing which a pendulum does. So, to work a pendulum, we must have a human body, an alive human body at that. You cannot tie a pendulum to a hook and expect it to work because there would be no source of current.

Nor would it be of much use if we could tie our pendulum to a hook and supply it with current because the current has to be in pulses varying according to the type of action desired. Just as in radio we have high notes, low notes, loud notes, and soft notes, so with a pendulum we must have the necessary current variation to do 'the necessary'.

Who is going to vary the current? Well, the Overself, of course. That is the brightest citizen we have around us, you know. After all, you who read this are just one-tenth conscious, so, knowing yourself, just think how brilliant you would be if you could call in the other nine-tenths of consciousness. You can certainly enlist its aid, the aid of the sub-conscious. The sub-conscious is brilliant; it knows everything that you have ever known, can do everything that you could ever do, and can remember every single incident since long before you were born. So if you could touch your sub-conscious you would get to know a very considerable amount of things, wouldn't you? You can touch your sub-conscious—with practice and with confidence.

The sub-conscious can also contact other sub-conscious minds. There are truthfully no limits to the powers of the sub-conscious mind and when the sub-conscious mind is allied to other sub-conscious minds, then indeed results may be achieved.

We cannot just ring up a telephone number and ask to speak to our sub-conscious because we have to look upon that Mind as being something like a very absent-minded professor who is

15

constantly sorting knowledge, storing knowledge, and acquiring knowledge. He is so busy that he can't bother with other people. If you pester him enough in the politest way, then he may answer your summons. So first of all you have to become familiar with your sub-conscious. You see, the whole thing is that the sub-conscious is the greater part of you, the much greater part of you, and I suggest that you give your sub-conscious a name. Call him or her whatever you like so long as it is a name agreeable to you. Supposing it is a male, then you could (purely as an illustration) use the name 'George'. Or if it is the sub-conscious of a female, then you could say 'Georgina'. But the whole point is that you must have some definite name which you link inseparably with your sub-conscious. So when you want to get in touch with your sub-conscious you could say for example, 'George, George, I want your help very much, I want you to work with me, I want you to——(here you specify what you want), and remember, George, that really we are all one and what you do for me you are also doing for yourself.' You need to repeat that slowly and carefully, and with very great thought. Repeat it three times.

The first time 'George' will probably shrug his mental shoulders and say, 'Oh that pestiferous fellow, bothering me again when I've got so much work to do,' and 'he' will turn back to his work. Next time you repeat it he will pay more attention because he is being bothered, but still he won't take any action. But if you repeat it a third time, 'George' or 'Peter' or 'Dave' or 'Bill' or whoever it is will get the idea that you are going to keep on until you get some action, so he will give a metaphorical sigh and help.

This is not fantasy, it's fact. I claim to know quite a lot about it because for more years than I care to remember I have done just this. My own sub-conscious is not called 'George', by the way, but a name which I do not reveal to anyone else just as you should not reveal to anyone else the name of your sub-conscious. Never laugh or joke about it because this is deadly serious. You are only one-tenth of a person, your sub-conscious is nine-tenths, so you have to show respect, you have to show affection, you have to show that you can be trusted because if you do not gain the co-operation of your sub-conscious then you won't do any of the things that I write about. But if you practise what you are reading, you can do the whole lot. So make friends with your sub-conscious. Give him or her a name, and be sure that you keep that name very, very private indeed.

You can talk to your sub-conscious. It is better if you talk slowly and repeat things. Imagine that you are telephoning someone on the other side of the world and the telephone line is a bit poor, you have to repeat yourself, you have quite a difficult time making yourself understood. Your listener at the other end of the telephone line is not an idiot for having difficulty in understanding your message, but general communications are bad, and if you overcome the difficulties of communications you can then find that you have a very intelligent conversationalist, one who is far more intelligent than you are!

When you are using the pendulum (we will go into that in more detail in a moment or so) you have to keep your feet flat on the ground so that the balls of your feet are in contact with the floor, and then you have to say something like, 'Sub-conscious (or the name you have chosen), I want to know what I must do to get success at such-and-such a thing. If you are going to make the pendulum work, will you make it swing backwards and forwards to indicate "yes", and from side to side to indicate "no" just as a human does when he nods for "yes" and shakes his head for "no".' You have to get over a message like that about three times, you have to explain very slowly, very clearly, and very carefully indeed what you want your sub-conscious to do and what you expect of the test because if you don't know what you want, then how can the sub-conscious give you any information? The sub-conscious won't know either. If you don't know what you want, you don't know when you've found it!

We started with dowsing, so let us deal first with what we call the dowsing pendulum. By the way, a little digression. Shall we refer to all sub-consciousness as 'George' for the purpose of this instruction? It's such a chore typing out 'sub-conscious' time after time, so we will just use the generic name of George in the same way as pilots call their automatic pilot 'Mike'. So George it is for our collective sub-conscious.

17

The dowsing pendulum should be a ball possibly an inch or an inch and a quarter in diameter. If you can get a very good wooden pendulum so much the better, or you may be able to obtain a 'neutral metal' one. But for the moment any pendulum will do as long as it is about an inch or an inch and a quarter in diameter. You should get a piece of thread such as boot-makers use for stitching on soles. I believe it's called cobblers' thread. You will need about five feet of it. Tie one end to your pendulum which should have a little eyelet on the top for that purpose, and tie the other end to a rod or even to an empty cotton reel. Then wind all the thread on to the cotton reel so that when you hold the small cotton reel in the palm of your hand the thread holding the pendulum is between the finger and thumb of your right hand—your right hand if you write with that one, but if you use your left hand instead, then, of course, the pendulum will be in the left hand. But first we have to sensitize or tune our pendulum for the particular type of material we wish to locate. Supposing we are going to look for a gold mine; first of all you get a little piece of sticky tape, about an inch long is sufficient, and then you put just a very small piece of gold (scraped from inside a ring, for instance) on to the sticky tape and then just lightly push it on to the pendulum. Then your pendulum has a piece of gold which will sensitize it to that metal, and when I say 'scrape' I mean that even if you get a grain, that will be adequate.

When you have that, put your ring, or another piece of gold, between your feet as you stand up. Stand with this gold, such as a gold ring or a gold watch, between your feet and slowly unwind the thread so that your pendulum lowers to perhaps a foot and a half from your fingers. At this point the pendulum should swing in a circular direction, that is, making a complete circle. If it does not do so, lower the thread a little or pull it up a little, the point being you have to ascertain the length of thread at which the pendulum swings most freely for gold. When you have determined that—it may be eighteen or twenty or twenty-two inches or similar—you make a knot in the thread and you write down the exact length, such as 'Knot One—Gold', and then you pull off your gold specimen with the Sellotape and pick up your watch or ring, and put a silver

18

article on the floor; it may be a coin or a piece of silver you have pinched from somebody else, but it must be silver. You also put a very fine scraping of silver on another piece of Sellotape and put that on to your pendulum. Then you try again to find what is the correct length for silver. When you have done that you make another note such as 'Knot Two—Silver'. You can go on doing it for different metals, and not only different metals but different substances. If you make a proper table, then you should have great fun 'prospecting'. Generally you will find that in terms of length the first thing to respond (at about twelve inches in length) is stonework. A bit longer thread, and you will get glass or chinaware. Longer still and you will get vegetable stuff. Go on increasing the length and you will get silver and lead, and then a bit further on you will find water. Longer still, you will find gold. Still longer, copper and brass. And the longest will be iron, and iron will be roughly just under thirty inches. So if you want to know what is beneath you, you just stand there and first of all think of whatever metal you are looking for. You adjust the length of your thread to the appropriate distance, and you very slowly walk forward.

Again—again—it is emphasized and re-emphasized that you *must* tell 'George' precisely what you are doing. You have to tell him that you want to prospect for gold, iron, silver, or whatever it is, and when he senses the radiations will he please swing the pendulum. At all times you must definitely keep thinking very strongly of that which you hope to find; otherwise, if you change over and think of something else, then you won't get it.

Apropos of this let me say that if you are looking for antique porcelain, for instance, and you suddenly think of women, then you will get the reaction for gold because the length of thread for gold and for women is precisely the same, and if a woman thinks about men she will get the reaction as if there was a diamond under the ground! That, of course, means that you will be completely misled. It would never do if you got the reaction for a diamond so you grabbed a shovel and pick and dug, but found instead a dead man. It could happen!

Now, it is advisable to use a shorter-cord pendulum for

19

everyday indoor use. After all, you don't want three, four, or five feet of thread getting tangled up every day. So when you are indoors use a separate pendulum. The pendulums which can be obtained commercially already have a thread or a chain attached to them, and frequently the chain is possibly six inches long, although the exact length varies, but that is of no moment.

Supose you want to find something—suppose you want to find out if a person is living in a certain area; then you sit down at a desk or table, but it must be an ordinary desk or table with no drawers or anything beneath because if you have anything beneath in, for example, a drawer, then the pendulum will be influenced by whatever is in the drawer. You may have a kitchen knife in the drawer. You may have a gold ring or something like that, and the pendulum, no matter how hard you think, will be influenced by the 'wrong' subject. So—sit at a plain table and have within arm's reach some sheets of ordinary plain white paper. Then you tell your pendulum, or rather you tell 'George', exactly what you want. You say, for example, 'Look, George, I want to find if Maria Bugsbottom lives in this area. If she does will you please nod by giving the pendulum a backwards and forwards movement, and if she does not will you please shake the pendulum from side to side.'

Then on the right-hand side of the table you have your piece of white paper, and on the top which is far away from you you put 'Yes', and on the bottom which is close to you you put 'Yes'. On the far left side of the paper you put 'No' and on the far right side you put 'No', and in the centre you put a little X to show that is the spot over which you are going to hold the pendulum. The pendulum, by the way, should be held about two inches above that X.

Sit comfortably. It doesn't matter if you have your shoes on or your shoes off, but you must have your feet on the floor, not on the bars of a chair—have them flat on the floor so that the balls of your feet are in contact with the floor. Then you get a map of the area desired and spread it to your left so that you have a white sheet of paper to the right and your map on the left. First you gently take the pendulum all over the area of the map, saying, 'Look, George, this is the area of my map. Is

Maria Bugsbottom anywhere within this area?' The pendulum is being taken over the map about two inches above the surface. When you have covered the whole area, you say, 'George, I am now going to start this investigation. Will you help me, George? Will you indicate "Yes" or "No" as the case may be?' Then (if you are right-handed) put your right elbow comfortably on the table and suspend your pendulum by its thread or chain, hold the thread or chain between your thumb and forefinger (the finger with which you point). See that the pendulum is about two inches above the X. Special note here —if you are left-handed everything will have to be reversed, but for the right-handed people in the majority—well, go by the instructions conveyed above.

Having got ready, and making sure that you are not likely to be disturbed, tell George that you are now ready to start work. Look at the map and put your left forefinger along the road on the map where you think Maria Bugsbottom may be living. Give an occasional glance at the pendulum. It may swing idly without any apparent sense, but if you get to where you believe your friend or enemy is living, then the pendulum will definitely indicate yea or nay.

It is a good idea to use a small-scale map first so that you can cover the biggest area, but when you get some sort of indication as if George was saying, 'Gee! This is a big area, I need to get closer than this,' then you get a large-scale map so that you can with practice locate any individual house.

After each test you definitely must replace your sheet of white paper by another—oh, you can use it for writing on; write letters on it or anything else, but only one sheet of white paper to one reading because you have impregnated that sheet with the impressions of whatever you are trying to find out so that if you try to repeat a reading, then the second reading will be influenced by the first and—well, that's all there is to it.

But no, perhaps that's not all there is to it after all because you've got to really frame your questions properly. George, you see, is a single-minded individual who can't take a joke and is extremely and exceptionally literal. So it's no good you saying, 'George, can you tell me if Maria Bugsbottom lives there?' If you ask a question like that the answer will be 'Yes',

21

because George can tell you if Maria Bugsbottom lives there, he *can*. And that is what you are asking. You are asking with a question in that form if the pendulum can tell you. You are not asking if she is actually living there at the moment. So whatever question you ask must be framed in such a way that George is not in a state of confusion.

The biggest difficulty about the whole affair is framing the questions so that they are fool proof, so that there are no double-meanings to them. In any question if you say, 'Can you tell me——?', then the answer will be Yes or No to the question of 'Can you tell me?' The other part of the question, 'if Maria Bugsbottom lives there?' will be unanswered because the first question will have swamped George's interest. So until you are more practised at this how about writing out your questions first and looking at your words to see if there is any way at all in which the question can be regarded as ambiguous or as having a double-meaning or is unclear. Let me repeat in big, bold, black capitals—YOU MUST BE SURE OF WHAT YOU ARE ASKING BEFORE YOU CAN POSE THE QUESTION.

Of course, when you have some practice it's quite easy to trace missing people. You have to have a small-scale and a large-scale map of the area in which the person is supposed to be missing. Then you have to be able to form some sort of mental picture of the person who is missing. Is it a big boy or a small girl? Is he or she ginger, blonde, or black-haired? What do you know about the person? You have to brief yourself as fully as possible, because, again, unless you know what you are seeking, then you don't know when you've found it.

It may happen at times when, for example, you are confined to bed, that you cannot stick your feet plunk on the ground. That is my trouble, so I have a metal wand about two and a half feet long, and I hold that in my left hand just like an antennae system to a portable radio, in fact that's what it is; it is an antenna rod from a portable radio. I pick up the wave from that in precisely the same manner as a more mobile person would with two flat feet.

When I am picking up impressions from a map or a letter, then I use a little propelling pencil, a metal one, and I touch the letter or the map and then the old pendulum starts to wobble and gives me an answer.

Never, never, never let anyone else touch your pendulum. It's got to be saturated with your own impressions. You should have several pendulums, one of wood, one of neutral metal, that is something like type-metal, and—well, you may want a glass one or you may want a plastic one, you may even have one which is hollow so you can put a specimen inside instead of sticking it up with Sellotape. But you will find one pendulum is more responsive than all the others for personal things, and you can make it even more responsive by carrying it on your person, getting it saturated with your own impressions. If you do that and never let another person use it or even touch it, then you will find you have something as potent and as useful as radar is to aircraft on a foggy night.

The pendulum cannot be wrong. George cannot be wrong. You can. You can go wrong with the form your questions take and your interpretations of the answers. Now, with computers one has to use a special language, otherwise the computer cannot make sense of what one is trying to get at, so pretend that your pendulum is a computer and frame your questions in such a clear one-way form that no possibility of error can occur because the pendulum can only indicate Yes or No. It can indicate uncertainty by doing a figure of eight. It can also indicate what sex a thing or a person is because most times for a man it can rotate in a right hand circle, clockwise that is, but for a woman it will rotate in a left-hand, anti-clockwise, circle. But if the man is very feminine then the poor old pendulum may go the wrong way, but it's not actually the wrong way, it is just indicating that the man isn't—he's more female and just has the necessary attachments, as one would say in the best circles, which would enable him to pass physiologically as a male specimen. All his thoughts may be female, so in that way the pendulum is far better as a judge than the best doctors!

Oh yes, I must be sure to tell you this; make sure your hands are clean before using the pendulum, otherwise, if, for instance, you have been gardening or stubbing out a cigarette butt in some poor plant's plant pot home, then you will get a reading for the soil content of the pores of your fingers. So be sure that your fingers and hands are clean. Be sure that your table is clean. It's no good, for instance, turning around and finding that a big fat cat is sitting on a sheet of white paper, and if it is then you have to use a different sheet of white paper!

With a pendulum and practice you can know how to dowse for minerals from a map. You go along looking for gold, if you like by having a little particle of gold attached to the pendulum. Then you let your finger go along the map to the location where you think there may be gold, and you think strongly of gold to the exclusion of all else. Or, if you are looking for silver, think strongly of silver to the exclusion of all else. All these things are very, very simple; until you get used to them you will be sure they are utterly impossible—they are not for you. But they are. It is only practice that makes a pilot able to take off in his aircraft and bring it down in one piece. It is only practice and faith in yourself that will enable you to go to your table, produce a map and a pendulum, and say, 'There—there is water, floods of it,' and then go to the actual site and find upon digging that the water is at a certain depth.

You can get a good idea of the depth of a thing by the strength of the oscillation or movement of the pendulum. This is not a book on pendulums or dowsing, but practice will soon teach you how to shorten or lengthen the chain or string, and how to gauge depth. But remember again that you must very definitely and strongly concentrate on that which you want to find or know.

You can also find out a lot about a person by using a pendulum over the signature on the letter. It is quite a useful exercise. But, remember, you must be sure of what you want to know, you must be sure of what you are asking, because if you are asking a thing in two parts then George is sure to answer the wrong one! And be very certain that you tell your subconscious—George or whatever you call him or her—precisely what you are trying to find out and what you expect the pendulum to do to indicate the information you desire.

Since writing the above I have 'tried it on the dog' because it seemed clear enough to me, but then I know it all, so I got someone who did not know it all to read it and now I am going to give some supplementary information.

'Well, how does one hold this pendulum?'

One rests one's elbow on the table, as already stated, and it should be the right elbow for a right-handed person and the left elbow for a left-handed person. Then you bend your arm so that your hand is at such a height from the table that your pendulum, which is suspended at the end of its chain, rests about two inches above the surface of the table. You actually hold the chain, string, cord, or whatever it is between your thumb and forefinger, and if you want to shorten the chain an inch or so in order to get a better swing—well, do so. Always adjust the length of the chain or thread between your finger and thumb so as to get the best swing or indication. Now, that should be clear enough—you just hold your forearm at such an angle that you are comfortable. You must be comfortable or you will not be able to do pendulum work. Similarly, if you have just had a heavy meal you will not be able to do pendulum work, or if you have something bothering you greatly unconnected with this pendulum, it will distract your attention. You must be in a fairly quiet state of mind, and you must be willing to work with the sub-conscious.

Now, I am also told, 'You've got me all confused; you say the Overself is going to vary the current—well, what is the connection between the Overself and the sub-conscious?'

Let us try to get this clear for ever and a day or a bit longer; there is you who is just one-tenth conscious. You are bottom man on the ladder, or you might even be bottom woman on the ladder. Above you you have your sub-conscious, and your sub-conscious is like the operator who controls the switchboard, etc., which is your brain. The sub-conscious is in touch with you through your brain—through your joint brain would perhaps be a better term—and the sub-conscious is also in touch with your Overself. So it's like you, the ordinary poor worker, who cannot get a word with the manager, you have to go through the shop steward or the foreman first. So you sort of hang around, try to make yourself obtrusive in the hope that the shop steward or the one above you will notice you, and wondering why the (you-know-what!) you are not at work will come and see what it's all about. Then you have to get your point of view over to the shop steward or foreman, and persuade him to take up your case with the manager or whoever is above him. This is similar to conditions with the Overself and you. Before you can get through to your Overself you have to enlist the aid of your sub-conscious, and once you can convince your sub-conscious that it's really necessary for your joint good, then the sub-conscious will contact the Overself and the pendulum will be varied according to the indications which you are 'perceiving'.

Incidentally, if you can get through to your Overself by way of the sub-conscious you can cure a lot of illnesses which you may have. The Overself is like the president of a company and he doesn't always know what minor ailments affect the lower departments. He knows it in times when conditions are very, very serious, but often he is in complete ignorance of some grievance which the lower order of workers have. But if you can get your shop steward to take up the matter with the Overself, or president, or general manager, then a grievance can be settled before it becomes serious. So if you have a persistent ache here, there, or somewhere else, then keep on at George or Georgina, say clearly what the trouble is, what is this pain, what does it feel like, why do you have it, and will the sub-conscious please see that you are cured. The Overself is the unapproachable. The sub-conscious is the link between you, the one-tenth conscious, and the Overself which is all conscious.

Oh sure, of course the pendulum can help you pick the winner of a race if you phrase your question sensibly, but look at this— 'Can you tell me who will win the two-thirty race?' Now what sort of a question is that? Look at it seriously and you will see that you are asking your sub-conscious to tell you this; can you, sub-conscious, tell me who will win the race? The answer, of course, would be 'Yes', and if you get a yes in answer to your question, you would think you were being fooled, wouldn't you? You can't do it that way at all.

Read back a bit to where I tell you how to locate things on a map. Now, in this case if you want to know who is going to win a certain race you will have to get a list of horses, the horses who are going to run in that specific race, and you will have to think definitely, 'Will this horse win?' And you will have to bring the pencil in your left hand slowly down to each name in turn, leaving it there about thirty seconds and thinking about that horse for about thirty seconds, asking if this horse will win the race. If the answer is 'No', then go on to the next horse until you've got to the one that is going to win. You can do it with practice. It's not very moral, you know, because betting and gambling are bad things, but anyway that is your own responsibility. I am just trying to make absolutely clear to you that you won't get any satisfactory result unless you quite definitely phrase your question in such a manner that there is only one question involved, a question which can be answered by a plain 'Yes' or a plain 'No'. I suggest you read that bit again because otherwise you are going to be really cross when you get a mixed up answer which really will be a mixed up questioner.

The last question here is, 'Yes, but where do I buy these pendulums?'

Actually they are fairly difficult to obtain because so many quick-money operators are out to make a fast buck and they are selling absolute junk, little things like key chain ornaments which they swear is a pendulum with your birthstone attached or something. But that is utterly useless. I am going to persuade Mr. Sowter to stock really reputable pendulums of a special type. There will be wooden ones and there will be neutral metal ones, and the metal ones will also have a recess or opening so one can place a specimen inside (such as a piece of hair picked up from a missing person's hairbrush or something like that). In that way the missing person can be missing no longer. Mr. Sowter of Touchstones of England will also be able to supply you with books. I will give you his address later, at the end of this chapter. But I do repeat again that it is utterly useless to buy a cheap little junk affair which is just a gimmick to get money out of your reluctant pocket. If you want a thing you have to pay for it, and a worthwhile pendulum will cost anything from $15 to $30, let's say in English terms from five to ten pounds. But you would pay that willingly for a small transistor radio, and a good pendulum is by far more useful to you than the aforementioned transistor radio. With a pendulum you can find a fortune—if you read this chapter properly and if you do really seriously practise.

Practice is the key to everything. You cannot be a great pianist unless you practise. The more important the pianist the more he or she practises—hours a day of those silly scales going 'bonk, bonk, bonk'. It is the same with a pendulum; you have to practise and practise and practise so you can do it by instinct, and you can practise with people's letters, with metals and all the rest of it, and that's the way you will make a success—practice.

Oh yes! There is one other little point which I should mention. I will mention it but, naturally, I would expect that the ordinary rules of politeness would apply; it is very, very important indeed that after you have used your pendulum you clasp it in your two hands to your forehead and then you solemnly thank George or Georgina for assisting you in this reading. 'Thank you' three times, do not forget that because if you do not thank 'him' or 'her' according to the elementary rules of politeness you may not get a response in two or three times hence, and—remember, your thanks must be repeated thrice just as your requests have been.

I am informed that there is some slight ambiguity in one part of this chapter (probably the whole thing is ambiguous but let's not dig up that problem). I am told that I do not make it clear how some poor wretch should stand when he or she is tuning the pendulum with a lump of gold or a crummy bit of silver between the feet. Okay, here it is again—you get your gold, silver, tin, lead, or copper and you put it on the ground between your feet. Then you stand upright with your spine straight and your left arm down by your side. Then you elevate your right hand so that your forearm is parallel to the ground and you see if that is a convenient method of doing it because if you brace your right elbow against your side you will not get undesired wobbles or squiggles in your pendulum but only what 'George' dictates. But the main thing, of course, is hold your arm at any distance convenient for you and convenient for the pendulum. And that's all there is to it!

You may obtain pendulums, books and other supplies from:

Mr. E. Z. Sowter,
Touchstones Ltd.,
33 Ashby Road,
Loughborough,
LEICESTERSHIRE, England.

CHAPTER TWO

Chill blew the wind. Icicles formed and hardened on projecting stonework. A skirl of dust around the concrete pillars, and the wind moaned off along the covered ways, keening a dirge to the departed sumer.

In the waterway named Bikersdike roaring ice-breakers heaved and groaned as they charged into the thickening ice. Charged and charged again; backing off cautiously along the just cleared channel, stopping, and *rushing* forward with great gouts of diesel fumes spraying from exhausts until the reluctant ice gave, protesting with sighs and a last long CRACK, followed by the grumbling crumble of fractured edges.

Shrouded figures bent listlessly over snow shovels, trying to spin out the time and still work hard enough to generate some heat. The wind freshened and wailed more sharply. As one the hooded men shouldered their shovels and shuffled off through the snow. A green shape momentarily hid the window and then blew away on the increasing gale; a garbage bag lifted bodily by the storm and strewn across the gardens.

The gloom deepened. Snow swirled more thickly around the hard-seen skyscrapers, blotting out the lights and turning the vista into a mysterious scene of shifting shadows and vague, ill-defined, pin-points of flickering lights. Motor traffic skidded from side to side and finally ground to a complete halt as the visibility lowered and lowered.

Snow fell, and fell, and fell. Throughout the night the mindless flakes came teeming down, twisting and eddying as though imbued with a crazy half-life. By morning, when the first faint glimmers of light struggled feebly through the opacity, the 'world' was at a standstill. Not a human, not a vehicle, not a bird broke the even shroud of freshly fallen snow.

Crack! A sharp, pistol-shot of sound rang out. The old man in the bed jumped and painfully turned round. A great split was growing across the floor-to-ceiling window pane. Warm in the room, and far, far colder than normal outside, and the glass had not been able to stand the temperature differential. Through the spreading crack the freezing air spewed into the room. Colder and colder dropped the temperature. The crack spread and spread, and widened. Soon the room was unusable.

The old man sat shivering in his wheelchair on the small gallery outside his door. All over the building-complex windows were shattering in the record cold.

The day seemed endless; the bitter cold seeped through the whole apartment. At the cracked window, where the freezing air streamed in, mounds of frost formed and fell as a white dusting on the floor.

The following day, after much persuasion, men came to replace the broken pane. The work of half a day, and the new glass was fitted. The men went to other apartments, where the windows had cracked. Slowly warmth returned to the rooms. Slowly the cats emerged from piled blankets which had been warmed by hot-water bottles.

Lower and lower dipped the temperature during the night. Suddenly, in the very early hours of the morning, a loud report awoke the old man. Horrified he watched, in the moon's pale glow, as the crack again spread all the way across the new foot pane of glass. Again the cold with frost forming in the room. And later in the day—the workmen found that the window frame was distorted, so there was nothing for it but to move to another apartment.

The days passed, and the weeks too, and at last the old man was again able to get on with his work. Answering questions, questions and *more* questions. As one lady wrote: 'It is *so* nice that I can write to you to get my questions answered. You charge nothing at all. But I don't ask Mr. XYZ any more as *he* charges fifty dollars a question!' Lucky Mr. XYZ, the old man thought, people don't even send *me* return postage!

But if some questions are answered in this book, then people will not have to write to me on the same things, right? So here are the questions *and* the answers.

Now here is a question from a woman who writes: 'What sort of adventure are you going to have when you have finished on this earth? Are you coming back to this world, or are you going to move to a different planet? I should be so interested to hear of your forthcoming adventures.'

Well, madam, my life is not an 'adventure'—it is hard work. Hard work fighting against bias, prejudice, and the hatred of people such as pressmen. You will find, if you study, that everyone without exception who has come to this Earth to do something special has been persecuted unmercifully by those who have no understanding. It reminds me that dogs bark at the heels of anyone who is strange. It reminds me that fleas can bite anyone irrespective of the status or stature of a person.

I do not live 'adventure'. I have been living, instead, in considerable hardship trying to do a specific task, and encountering all manner of quite unnecessary hindrances. So please do not write to me about 'adventures'. None of these have been such to me. They have been unnecessary suffering such as a well-intentioned teacher might suffer at the hands of unheeding, demented children.

When I leave this Earth I shall never at any time return to it, nor to this system. No doubt when I have passed on some stupid person will delude the credulous with advertisements in the occult papers claiming 'In direct touch with Lobsang Rampa—your questions answered from the Heavenly Fields'. Well, don't believe a word of that. I shall not be in this zone at all, and I tell you quite definitely that people who advertise saying they get direct information and answers from those who have passed over are not really doing themselves or the deceased a service. People who have passed over have another life to live, another task to do. If you, for instance, emigrated to a far distant country where communications were poor with the area you had just left, could you stop doing your new work just because some stupid dope in the 'old country' was saying, 'Oh, you must help me, I have advertised saying I am in direct touch with you—you must help me.' No, of course you wouldn't! You have your own work to do and you would not be interested in these advertisers who are just out to make money fast on the credulity of the average person.

When I have gone from this Earth, then, I shall have gone to a completely different zone. I know where I am going, I know what I am going to do. So when I have gone do not be deluded by stupid advertisements from stupid people in the press.

Here is a question: 'You say that there cannot be a positive without a negative, a good without an evil. Does this assertion hold true in some or all dimensions for some or all of time? Will not God eventually illuminate the darkness everywhere by the sheer power of His love? Or will there always, somewhere on the outside, be an unending blackness or vacuum for God to light up and fill with His positive embrace?'

The Christian 'belief' as taught nowadays is not at all as Christ Himself taught. Various priests throughout the ages have messed about with the teachings and the translations to get a bit more power for themselves.

Of course there cannot be a positive without a negative. It is absolutely clear. All life consists of impulses, vibrations, electric currents if you like, and you try to get your radio to work when you only have one wire connected to the plug. It cannot be done. Or if you prefer a non-electrical system you try to get a bath tap to run when there is nothing else coming into the system—you will soon find there is no water left. A positive and a negative are utterly essential, otherwise there cannot be any 'flow' and it is so stupid to think that God is some old geezer who goes about with a flashlight in His hand lighting up dark places. It isn't God who does it, it is the people who live in the places, light or dark. On Earth, for instance, the majority of people are busily engaged in cutting each other's throats behind their backs or doing whatever harm they can. This is the Age of 'pulling down'. You get cheap morons pulling down people like Churchill and other great men because it makes the cheap punks feel great; it makes them think, 'Oh, he's only human like us, he can fall down too.'

Christians always imagine that there is no other form of religion except Christianity, they always imagine that the

33

Christian God goes about with a flashlight in each hand and perhaps a few candles in His mouth trying to illuminate the ways of the heathen who were managing quite well before Christianity started. Furthermore, Christianity is merely a hotch-potch of Hinduism, Buddhism, the Jewish faith, etc., all cooked up to suit a different time and age. So please do not write such a lot of rot about God lighting up and embracing everyone everwhere. It just doesn't happen that way.

The questioner goes on: 'As soon as Prince Satan is banished by the bright glare of His love will he then just retreat, bringing his darkness with him into the unending space and time? Will he, at some time, find it to his advantage to unite with the Creator in perfect balance and harmony, or is he for ever committed to defying the will of God?'

You *must* have a positive and a negative, you cannot have just one, and there is no possibility of 'Satan' running hell for leather, or should it be 'leather for hell?' to get out of the way of some imaginary God who is hot in pursuit. If such a thing could happen there would be stasis—a state where everything was stationary, where nothing could move. I repeat again that you have to have a positive and a negative, and one is as important as the other. If you do not have a negative then you can't have a positive, and that's all there is to it.

This person says: 'There was a war in the heavens, thereby leaving open the possibility that there was once a complete unity of all and everything with no conflict between positive and negative. If so is this conflict now irrevocable?'

But, my dear madam, it is not a conflict in the connotation of a good guy and a bad guy knocking lumps off each other. It is not like that at all. You take a battery and a bulb. You've got your battery—flashlight, if you like—and when you switch on (read this carefully) you just complete the circuit so that positive and negative are connected to the bulb and so you get a light. So if you go and bump off old Satan, or negative, whichever way you like to call it, then the light stops, everything stops, and before too long, with nothing to do, the poor old battery decays and goes dead. Try it yourself and see. Go out to a store somewhere, buy a battery—perhaps a $4\frac{1}{2}$-volt battery—and buy two lumps of wire, perhaps two feet long each, and then get a bulb. Connect up the battery and the bulb, and you will have light. Disconnect the negative and you won't have any light, and that is all there is to it. This 'never-ending struggle' is the struggle of life itself. A baby struggles to get out of its mother, it struggles against illness, it struggles against cramps as it is growing, it struggles when the teeth are coming through—and makes a horrible noise in the process of struggling!—and all through the life there is struggle. Struggle to get a partner, struggle to get divorced from the partner, struggle to get a job, struggle to knock out the boss above so that promotion may be gained. Oh no, there must be struggle! It doesn't matter what you do, you still have to struggle, you even have to struggle out of bed in the mornings!

When struggle ends life ends. When life ends on this Earth, then you go to another existence and you start struggling all over again. You might struggle in a more gentlemanly or lady-like manner on another world, but it is still struggle, get that clear.

Our enquirer goes on: 'Initially I am distressed at the prospect of a never-ending struggle between an ecstatic happiness and an empty despair, with no anticipation of its resolve into a final happy ending even though it be trillions of eons in the future. But as in the case of exploring into and analysing other truths which at first alarmed me, I am of the firm conviction that the truth shall make one free in the final outcome, no matter what it is.'

Well, there it is, I am telling you the truth. I tell you the truth in all my books so if you believe me you would have known the truth before this. The truth is this; we are all struggling upwards to a final goal. That final goal is not sitting around like a crowd of hippies with some larger-than life God decorated in gold and poster colours parading before one. God is quite a different thing from that. God is utterly different from the average Christian conception. As the Christians visualize 'God' it's just a parody of what the ancient 'heathens' visualized as the Gods on Olympus. They thought of Jupiter and a bunch of other Gods and Goddesses, all making merry on the top of some mythical mountain. They must have been mighty cold up there, that's all I can say, because the imaginary pictures of them show them as being remarkably poorly clad and if they had ever cavorted on the top of a mountain in that lack of clothing then they would need to keep cavorting to keep warm. But, anyway, this is the way it is:

Let us get rid of bias first, and let us look at the real problem, let us look at Communism; a certain little gang of people at the start thought, 'Oh! why should this group of people have everything? We are the workers, we want everything too.' And so they ganged up and they formulated some sort of a policy. The Communist thought that all men and women should be equal and everyone should have the same amount of money, forgetting that if all the world had the same amount of money today they would all have different amounts tomorrow. But the Communists didn't like the way the 'Capitalists' were going on so they formulated some kind of policy—if it can be termed policy—in which all the values of the Capitalist were completely reversed, and then they went out to get converts, even if it made them out of work, even if they starved to death from hunger, and even if it brought misery to the world.

In the early days of the Romans and the Greeks and a few other assorted people there was a very good religion, a very good code of living, and people were happy, much more so than they are now. For example, there was much more freedom, cleaner freedom, in sex. There was much greater companionship, comradeship, between men and women, but then a little gang of people were jealous of the way the Greeks, the Romans and assorted other races were going on; they were too happy to be natural, they thought. So they took the Teachings of a great man and altered them, bent them around, twisted them in a circle, and reversed everything that the Romans, the Greeks, etc., had been doing. Sex became something despicably filthy, and sex was awarded only to men as an inducement to do certain things which the priests wanted them to do. Women, instead of being the equal of men as they had been in the days of the Romans and the Greeks, women were now slaves, chattels, baggages for men to do with as they wished. But you often get situations like that when these little groups, possibly homosexuals at that, took a dislike to anyone. And so throughout the years Christians have worked hard to get converts, and they were going to make converts even if it killed the human concerned. If you think that is strange, then remember the Crusades; armed bands of brigands invading other peoples who were peacefully inclined. If you want further food for thought think about the Spanish Inquisition where they 'tortured a man to save his soul'. What a stupid lot of rot! If I see one side of a coin that is what I see, but a person looking at the obverse of the coin would see a different picture altogether. It is the same coin but we have different viewpoints.

And all this talk about exploring other 'truths'. The truth is that humans are upon this Earth to grow, to develop into more spiritual creatures, and if they do not do it they will be removed and other creatures will be put here. It is like plants in a garden; a gardener plants a whole bunch of plants and watches them carefully, and if they do not develop as they should then they are pulled out and fresh plants of a different type are put in. That is all humans are, that is all horses are, pigs are the same; different plants, different growths, different things which are being observed upon this Earth.

Our querist goes on: 'If such a thing as a perfect, final peace were to come about in the worlds of rational beings would the opposite worlds then be doomed to an opposite fate, to so-called hell for ever, or would their outcome, more hopefully, be also one of a kind of peace that manifests itself somehow in an opposite manner, whatever that might be? Will not all Gods, intelligent, rational beings some day learn all their necessary lessons once and for all and return to a complete awareness of and oneness with the Creator? Or would it always be in His scheme of infinite love to be continually creating new beings who can choose to give themselves to Him, after first undergoing great struggle between positive (good) and negative (evil) forces? Then, after they have passed all their tests and returned to God will they be followed by other new created beings in a never-ending creation?'

If 'peace' comes to this world, perfect peace, that is, then it would mean that people here would not have to come back again, they would have learned a lesson, the lesson of keeping the peace, and then they would move on to some higher state of evolution where they could go to school again and learn something else. But all this about 'returning to God' is nonsense. You don't return to God at the end of this life on Earth just as a small child returns to Daddy or Mummy. It is not like that at all. There are many, many things to be learned. There are billions, trillions of years to live in different stages, and I must tell you in this connection that I had a most offensive letter from two people in Australia. A man and a woman claimed that they were 'in touch with the Gardeners of the Earth', and the Gardeners of the Earth were such wonderfully good people, and all I write in 'The Hermit' must obviously be imagination because the Gardeners of the Earth would never do anything to harm a human. My goodness me! These people in Australia—they must have a hole in their head or something! Humanity is not the highest form of creation, it is just another specimen the same as an ant is a specimen, the same as a tapeworm is a specimen. A tapeworm is learning one thing, a human is learning another, or rather—correction—they should be learning, which is a different matter altogether.

But again, let me state definitely that we are here to learn certain things and to do certain things, and life goes on and on in cycles. I prefer to regard it as the swing of the pendulum; we have a pendulum swinging, now it is at the top of its stroke and we are at a Golden Age where everything is wonderful, everything is peaceful—but where nobody learns. And then the pendulum falls and things become worse and worse, lower and lower. When we reach the lowest point of the pendulum swing there are wars and rumours of wars, murders, everything, the whole crime calendar rolled into one. But after that the heedless pendulum continues upwards and so we get a Golden Age again wherein no one learns for it is a fact, a sad fact but still a fact, that people only learn by hardship and by suffering, and when a person has all that he wants he sits back and enjoys comfort and does not do anything to try to help others or even himself.

Another person writes to ask: 'Can we ever meet our individual opposites?' By that, presumably, is meant the twinsoul, and if that should be so then the answer is no, you do not meet your twinsoul on this world because if you did you would be complete and thus could not stay here. You can only stay here if you have an 'anchor' which moors you here, some defect, or some artificially induced fault which enables one to stay here. People who come from beyond the spheres are like divers, they have to wear the equivalent of a lead belt, lead boots, etc., in order to keep submerged in this dreary world. So if a person met his or her twinsoul there would be the nearest approach there can be to perfection, and you cannot have perfection in a world such as this. So you will have to wait for your twinsoul until you leave this world.

Now another person says: 'You emphatically declare that each one of us finds God alone through individual effort, and that we should not depend upon others for assistance. Do you mean that the ultimate responsibility for use of one's freewill in committing oneself to God rests squarely upon each individual's shoulders, no matter what kind or unkind things have been done to us by others one consciously chooses the direction of his vision. Of course truth and justice or deceit and injustice can affect the course of our lives either way towards or away from the light, but isn't the application of the Golden Rule vitally important for each of us to practise, thereby helping others?'

I say quite definitely that every person must stand alone. It is silly to join cults, gangs, associations, institutes, etc., etc., and to expect 'salvation' thereby because you won't find salvation in these money-making cults which are merely out to—get your money! Look at it like this; a person dies—leaves this Earth for the astral realms—and that person is going to go to the Hall of Memories and answer to himself or herself for things which have been done or have not been done. There is no one else there except the newly arrived soul or entity or whatever you like to call it and the connection with the Overself. Now, I tell you quite definitely—quite, quite definitely—you answer alone. You won't get the secretary or chief tutor of the Hot Dog Society, or whatever you like to call all these cult things, to come and answer for you. You won't find the President of the Rednose Association coming and saying, 'Oh yes, Overself, you don't know anything; I told this person to do such a thing because the rules of our Association say that that is so, so he should take your place.'

You have to stand alone, then, naked and probably ashamed with it. And if you toss out all thoughts of these associations and cults on this Earth, then you will be in training to answer alone when you reach the Other Side.

Of course, if you are going to answer to your Overself then you need to have some good answers, and the best way is to obey the Golden Rule which is, Do unto others as you would have them do unto you. This person who writes this question seems to be wriggling and writhing and doing anything to evade the simple truth, the truth which is—you have to learn to stand on your own two feet, no matter whether they are flat or not. You have to stand on them, you have to be responsible for yourself, and if you help others by adherence to and obedience of the Golden Rule, then you will have much good in your astral bank account.

Let me again state that God is not standing there with a whacking great cane, and the devil is not standing there with branding irons either. God is a positive force, the devil is a negative force, they are not people who praise or torture. While down here on this Earth you cannot understand things which happen in many more dimensions. In the same way a sea slug sitting on a bit of slime in the bottom of the ocean could not possibly understand what people on the Moon are experiencing, it could not even understand what people in high-rise buildings are thinking or doing, nor could it understand the commotion which is caused when people turn their television sets full on. All that would be completely beyond the comprehension of people here in the third dimension to try to understand what people in the ninth, tenth, eleventh, or twentieth dimension are doing. So everything is relative. We might understand more or less what other people on Earth are doing, we might have a greater feeling that they are doing right or they are doing wrong, but how could we possibly attempt to understand what twentieth-dimension people are doing? You cannot comprehend the concepts of another dimension unless you have had some experience of that dimension.

Actually you can get an idea, a rough idea, from thinking that everything is vibration. One end we call 'feel', a bit further we say 'sound', higher up still it is 'sight'. Everything is vibration, on any planet, on any system, or any universe, so that gives us some faint illustration of other dimensions. It is rare indeed for a person to feel a sound or see a sound, yet they are all vibrations, all part of the same scale. There are entities who can see sound, there are animals who can hear different sounds, those which are beyond human range. Dogs, for instance, will respond to a whistle which is completely silent to humans. Cats see colours on a different spectrum; cats, for example, see red as silver. But to give another slight illustration which might help, try to work out this for yourself:

We have a person who was born blind. Now, you have the task of explaining to that person who was born blind the difference between red and pink, or between yellow and orange. How are you going to do that? You can't. There is no way in which you can explain to a blind person the difference between yellow and orange, or amber and brown. You could possibly explain the difference between red and green if the person was extremely sensitive and could *feel* the difference. But you work that out—you want to know what other dimensions are like, so cut off a dimension that you know, cut off sight. Then how are you going to explain to a person who has never known sight the difference between pink and red?

Supposing you have a person who is completely deaf; how are you going to get that person to appreciate the difference between two fairly similar musical notes? Not so easy, eh? So unless you can give me answers to *my* questions I cannot tell you of the experiences of the ninth dimension.

Here is a question which will make your hair stand on end, so ladies, put on your bath hats; gentlemen, if you are bald, your hair will be standing up on your bald skulls! Here is the question: 'According to the Zen philosophers there really is no right or wrong thereby eliminating the need for judgment.'

Can you answer that? Well, I see the point behind it, and the answer is this: on the Greater scale of things 'right' and 'wrong' are completely different from what they are on Earth. Here there are certain rules or laws which have to be obeyed for what is commonly thought of as the common good. For example, it is not right to steal, so a man, in theory at least,

41

should starve to death rather than steal money to buy food.

If a man is smoking and for some reason he puts his still alight pipe in his trousers pocket and sets his trousers on fire, then in theory he shouldn't pull them off because then he would be naked and he would offend public decency, and he could in fact be charged with 'indecent exposure'. So, according to law, a man should be definitely hotted up in all the best places rather than expose himself to the lewd gaze when his trousers were on fire. Which do you consider right?

While on the subject of indecencies, in some places the lady must keep her face covered from the gaze of all mankind. She can leave the lower part of her body quite uncovered and still be decent. Yet in other parts of the world she can have her face bare but the lower part of her body must be covered, otherwise she is very much in disgrace. So what is right in one part of the world is wrong in another. Right and wrong are man-made precepts, and these have no basis of stability beyond the Earth. At the same time, if one is judging oneself in the Hall of Memories one has had to go according to the rules in force during one's lifetime. It would not matter in the least if you had transgressed against the purely artificial laws, for instance, if you had removed your clothes in public—that would not be an offence in the Greater Reality of the astral world. Anyway, Christians believe that Man is made in the image of God and yet they make an awful hullabaloo if a person appears naked, but why? Are they saying that God is indecent? But anyway, that is just a personal thought of mine.

What does matter in one's 'judgment' is that you have to answer—Have you harmed another person? Have you helped another person? As examples of this, a person had a job which you coveted. You very much wanted that job, you could see yourself exactly fitting into that position, and so you made a little plot against the incumbent of that position so that he was discharged from his employment and you took it in his place. Now that, of course, is a sin, because that is going against a law of the Universe which is 'Do no harm unto others'. But if you told a little white lie in order to help a person get a job which he really could do, then that lie would not be an offence, it would be good!

42

Far away, above all the trumpery laws and regulations of mankind, there are basic truths, basic rules which we transgress only at our peril. The laws of Man on Earth are not made for the individual but for the majority, and so that the best interests of a majority can be served often a law will appear to inflict hardship upon the individual. Never mind, that is one of the things we have to put up with if we are crazy enough to live in communities because liberty is a relative term. If we were free to do anything at all then we could go into anyone's house, take anything we wanted, do anything we wanted, and then we would be entirely 'free'. Actually, that would not be to the benefit of the community as a whole and so there are laws to protect the majority against the minority, and we break those laws at our peril, peril on Earth, that is; most of them don't matter the slightest beyond this Earth. What does it matter, for instance, if a person buys a packet of cigarettes in England after eight o'clock in the evening? What does it matter if, in Canada, a person buys a newspaper on a Sunday? All these are childish stupid things, but somebody had an idea somewhere even if nobody knows what the sense of the said law now is!

Here is another question: 'I understand that entities of the fourth and other dimensions are all very busily occupied in helping souls in this, the third dimension, and they stay exclusively helping us upon this world. What do they get out of it?'

No, of course that is not true! Let us consider life, all life, as a school—of course somebody will write to me and say, 'Oh, you are repeating yourself, you've told us all this before.' But obviously I couldn't have told it very clearly or people wouldn't still be asking me about it, so you people who want to write and complain, just be quiet for a bit, will you?

All life is a school, then. Different classes, different grades. We on this Earth happen to be in Grade Three (third dimension). People in the fourth dimension are in Grade Four. People in the fifth dimension are in Grade Five. Now tell me seriously, thinking back to your own school days, can you truthfully say that the students in Grade Five at your school were very interested in staying on and helping the students in

Grade Three? More likely the Grade Five students thought the Grade Three students were crummy little punks who were beneath even a contemptuous notice. That is so, isn't it? So let me tell you this: there are certain people who are teachers who are unfortunate enough to be persuaded to 'volunteer' to come to Grade Three to teach the crummy little punks in this class, and when they get down to Grade Three they find that the students are not at all anxious to learn (were *you* anxious to learn when you were at school?), so the teacher gets all sorts of nasty things said about him and eventually he gets really fed up with the whole procedure, and he says to the Headmaster, 'Well Boss, I can't stick all these punks, I have to go to a different class or I shall go even crazier. Where can you move me?'

So take it from me, the teachers on the Earth—teachers from other dimensions—are trying hard to do something to help the people in Grade Three, help the people in the third dimension. And if the people in the third dimension would be a bit more appreciative they would get on much faster because there comes a time when even the best of teachers get sick and tired of continual persecution and wants to move on.

Now I have been taken to task, not for the first time and not for the last, but I have had a comment: 'Oh, but you can't leave it like *that*! ! People will not at all understand what you mean by 'God'. In some places you say that God is a concept and in other places you say that God is a person. How are you going to account for that?'

Oh dear, oh dear, troubles never come singly, do they? Well, there are Gods and Gods. The average person prays to his or her 'God'. Actually the prayers are going on the first-class route to the Overself, but if you want to get a bit higher up then you can pray to the Manu of the planet. Or, if you have 'connections' up there, you can pray to the Manu of this whole Universe. As I have tried to make clear in my books (apparently without any success!) the God-system is very much like a multiple store or a chain of stores where you have each branch manager as 'God' to his cohorts or hirelings. But all the departmental managers or branch managers look upon the President or Chairman of the Company as 'God'. So let's try to get this clear; one can pray to a person whom one re-gards as 'God'. He may be the Overself, he may be a Manu, or he may be a Chief Manu, or he may even be the God of the Universe. But he is not the 'top God' by any means. The 'top God' is something completely different, something which one can only regard as a concept at the present time because, as I have already been telling you, you cannot discuss, nine or ten or twenty dimensional things in three-dimensional concepts. So go on regarding your God as a person or entity, but keeping clear in your mind that there is something very, very much higher than all this.

CHAPTER THREE

The Most Honest Man in Montreal stood square behind his shuttered door and peered through a crack at the scene outside. The street was like a battlefield; police cars and motor-cycles roared around. Bottles and rocks flew through the air, landing with a satisfying 'crunch'. Across the road from the store where Hy Mendelson stood on guard over Simons Cameras, the great embattled premises of La Presse loomed as a symbol of might of the Press.

Yes—the striking pressmen had brought the great roaring machines to a halt. No longer did the ticker-tape spew out miles of messages. No longer did yammering reporters hound those who were deemed 'newsworthy'. The press strike was a time when, for some, the 'air was cleaner—may the strike long continue!'

But for people like Hy Mendelson, boss of Simons Cameras, the loss of business was great and serious. Behind his store a new through-way road was being cut. In front of him—the La Presse strikers, police, barricades, all the impediments to honest trade. (Now, of course, the strike is over—and Hy Mendelson is prospering again!)

Why do we have to have strikes when so many people are out of work? If people aren't satisfied, then let them give up their jobs to those who will do the work. Why blackmail a whole country, a whole *continent* just at the whim of a few money-hungry leaders of Communist-inspired unions? The Press—and the unions—the curses of modern day life!

Hy Mendelson, a good man, an honest man. Why should he and others like him be almost ruined by fighting strikers? If it is not embattled pressmen stopping trade on the street, then it

46

is striking mailmen preventing him from running his very efficient mail-order business. I have known him for years; he is a good friend of mine, and I feel strongly that all these vicious strikes should so harm the innocent and just.

Montreal was like a beleaguered city. Roaming strikers, very efficient police, and gangs of would-be revolutionaries lounging insolently on street corners. Long-haired men revelling in their dirt and deliberately torn rags swaggered along the streets muttering outlandish and uncouth greetings to others of their ilk whom they met briefly and passed on.

Montreal, where French-Canadians did not like French-Canadians! Where it was frequently very difficult (as I found) to get any attention in a French-Canadian store unless one spoke French. The City of Two Tongues, a city which I found it delightful to leave when the time came for that action as you will read later.

The old man often watched from his home in the river. Watched the flash of explosions by night. Watched the flashing light of police cars in pursuit of arsonists, revolutionaries, watched the F.L.Q. crisis where a good and just man was murdered at the behest of some illiterate punk.

Watched too, when Mayor Drapeau came by. Mayor Drapeau, one of the finest, if not *the* finest, man French-Canada has produced. Mayor Drapeau, who is so hounded by a Press with no understanding nor conception of Greatness. For it is truly a fact that Mayor Drapeau has made Montreal into a *city*, instead of the collection of hovels it was before his advent. Yes, His Worship is one of the truly Great in this age of very very little men.

The old man in the wheelchair watched when the F.L.Q. hoodlums went rushing by his window, escorted by grim police, when they were taking Diplomat Cross to the 'foreign territory' of the Cuban Pavilion on the site of Man and His World. The helicopter that took these gangsters off to the airport flew over the old man's head.

But now, in the gathering dusk, the old man lay upon his bed watching the lights of Monteal come on. The first dull glow of the newly switched-on street lamps as they burned dull first, then quickened into yellow-green light. The multi-

47

coloured neons on the advertising signs and the tall skyscrapers as they suddenly blazed into the light of night life. Way up on Mount Royal the great metal Cross stood limned in light against the darkening sky as somewhere a robot sensor responded to the stimulus of darkness and turned on a switch.

Downriver, beneath the fairy tracery of the Jacques Cartier Bridge, a liner came steaming along all aglow with strings of lights twinkling from forepeak to mastheads to sternpost and jackstaff. Little tugs, with sides beribboned with lights, fussed around the ocean giant while from them came shouts in the peculiar *patois* which the French-Canadian believes is French.

Gliding lights in the night sky and the muted roar of jets showed the arrival of aircraft from the capitals of the world. Sabena from the Belgian cities, Lufthansa, K.L.M., and the streaming crowds from Britain. There came too a plane from Russia, a rarity which now is a rarity no longer. The aircraft of the nations of the world flew overhead. Now, though, an increasing number flew non-stop to Toronto to avoid the inconvenience and rudeness at the airport of the City of Two Tongues!

But the hours crept slowly by. Lights changed. Fresh ones were lit, others were extinguished. Traffic on the roads slowed, but never stopped, for this city never slept. The old man turned, glanced without affection at the pile of letters yet to be answered, and mentally consigned them to a warmer place. Tomorrow, he thought, he would start early and clear up the lot before the next day's bunch arrived.

So thinking, he turned over and went to sleep. Others in the house may say that he snores like a grunting pig with the overtones of a rusty gate, but when one is astral travelling—well, one is entitled to snore!

Morning came as morning will in even the best regulated of households. Morning came, and with it came the time, once again, for work, the never-ending drudgery of letters, letters, letters.

Here is a question which is very topical because acupuncture is very very much in the news at present. The questioner writes: 'I have read so much about the wonders of acupuncture, yet no one seems to be able to explain exactly why it

works. Could the twelve major areas of insertion of the
correspond to twelve psychic centres of the body, thus ex]
ing the 'mystery' and perhaps providing a link between
third and fourth dimension of existence?'

Yes, there is so much mystery about acupuncture. Unfortunately the Press have over-dramatized things. Acupuncture is
far more effective in the Far East than it is in the Western
world. Now, the reason for that is not difficult to seek.

I repeatedly state the truth that humans are just puppets of
the Overself. All right, when was the last time you went to a
puppet show? Have you ever had a puppet in your hands?
Even the simplest of puppets have a string which controls the
head, other strings control the arms and the legs, so even the
simplest of puppets has five controlling strings. How many
more strings then, can a human, which is quite a complicated
sort of puppet after all, have?

Acupuncture works by intercepting a nerve stream, by short-
ing out a nerve stream which has some defect. For example,
you might have a car and you find that you cannot use it
because every time you switch on the ignition and associated
circuits the fuse blows, and you cannot exactly find out what is
wrong with the car. So, if you do not have all the time in the
world to spare, you locate the area in which the trouble occurs.
It might be (purely for example) the horn which has a defect,
so if you cut out the horn for the time being you can drive your
car and go to a garage where the car can be repaired.

The acupuncture process temporarily shorts out a defective
part of the nervous system and causes a stimulation to go in a
reverse direction which causes very considerable alleviation of
the condition giving distress.

We have our puppet; the puppet strings go to the hand of
the operator, but the hand of the operator is controlled by the
brain of the operator, and so if the puppet does not manage too
well it may be that the hand of the operator cannot manage to
carry out the commands of the brain. Now, let us replace that;
let us say the puppet is a human, the hand is the brain of the
human, and then we can see that if the brain cannot give the
right messages to any limb or portion of the body then a dys-
function occurs, and if it is in an ordinary puppet then possibly

49

a string could be lengthened or shortened to carry out a temporary repair. We do the same type of thing, in principle at least, with acupuncture.

But why does it work better with the Easterner? Well, the Easterner has a different set of vibrations from the Westerner. The Easterner is more concerned about the things of the spirit, more concerned about the life after death, more concerned about moral values, ethics, and all that. So the Easterner is more able to accept the reality that sticking a needle or two into one's shuddering anatomy can cause a dramatic decrease in the physical symptoms.

The Western world is more concerned about the things of this life, more concerned about getting power over others, more concerned about making money in a hurry and not parting with it except for one's own creature comforts.

The Western world is not able to believe anything unless they can get hold of it and tear it to pieces, and when they have utterly destroyed it say: 'Well, fancy that! It did work after all. Too bad it was destroyed in proving it was right!'

I believe even the Christian Bible has something to the effect that unless one be as a little child one cannot enter into the Kingdom of Heaven. All right: Unless one can have a childlike simplicity and a true faith that there are things which humans on Earth cannot explain, then one will not be benefitted by acupuncture!

Acupuncture is not a faith healing thing at all, there is no faith in it because acupuncture really does cure. But first you have to have the metabolism of a sensitive person who can accept the reality that a cure is going to be effected. Now, that is different from faith healing. Some people say: 'Well, you prove that to me and I still won't believe it.' (Like the old woman who went to the Zoo and saw a giraffe and exclaimed, 'Gee, there ain't no such animile!') So—no matter how good the acupuncturist, no matter how brilliant his needles, unless the person who is to be treated has the necessary spiritual apperception a cure will not occur, and the Press hearing of such a case will eagerly rush into print and thoroughly discourage and lower the perception point of others who could, without Press intervention, have been cured.

50

Now, here is a nice little question which also, undoubtedly, is in the minds of many people. The question is: 'Does one ever have to return to, say, the fourth or third, or even the second or first dimensions after having existed somewhere in the fifth through the ninth dimensions for reasons of having led a wantonly evil life in one of these higher planes?'

The answer to that is a very definite *no*! If a person is a Naughty Boy in the third dimension he comes back to the third dimension, he does not go to the second. I believe you get the same sort of system in schools; if a student doesn't do his work very well while he is in Grade Three then at the end of term he goes on vacation and has an unpleasant interview with his parents, at the end of the vacation he goes back to school in Grade Three; he doesn't get shoved down to Grade One.

In the same way a person struggling along through the School of Evolution does not come back to a lower Grade but only to the same Grade. So if you misbehave or do not learn your lessons properly, then you will be coming back to this poor sorry old Earth again where conditions are going to be a bit worse for quite a long time.

People come down to lower dimensions for special purposes; they are volunteers (do you remember the old army story of volunteers—the Sergeant says: "Hey you, I want ten volunteers—you, you, and you!') Well, perhaps people in much higher dimensions take a look at the Earth and shudder at what they see. Then they go back and come to the conclusion that someone—some specialist—will have to return to the Earth as a volunteer and find out what is wrong, and then help the people of the Earth get on the right path.

There are a few snags attached to that because one of the greatest laws is that you cannot use for your own gain knowledge which you have acquired in a different dimension, you have to live as a denizen of the third dimension, or whatever it is, and make do with the facilities inherent to the third dimension.

Another usual reaction is that the volunteer is 'different' so he or she is persecuted and, all too frequently, disliked because the person is, in effect, a foreign body, a splinter in the body of the Earth. You, for instance, if you get a splinter stuck in any

51

part of your anatomy—well, you make quite a commotion until the splinter is dug out. The volunteers have also the painful experience of finding that they are not popular. It doesn't matter who they are. Even Christ was persecuted. Even Gautama was persecuted. Even Moses had more than he could deal with. And during their lifetime they were not popular, they were regarded as nosey-parkers, as do-gooders, etc., etc. Only after such a volunteer has been gone from the Earth plane for many years does it dawn on the Earth people that—oh well, the person must have been some good after all, and then they write a Bible or two about him. But that doesn't help the volunteer very much, does it?

At the present stage the poor wretched volunteers have a further hazard to the success of their work; the pressmen are always looking out for anyone who is 'different', and if a person is 'different' he doesn't 'play ball' with the Press and so he gets persecuted and he is called a fake, and that further inhibits the success of what he is trying to do. He may, for instance, be doing very well indeed at his voluntary task, but then some crummy pressman cooks up an entirely imaginary story together with 'documentary proofs' and that really does cause a very considerable obstacle to a good task.

There is another question which fits in well here. The question is: 'Having achieved the ninth dimension, is one crystallized to become one for ever with the Creator irrevocably and for ever and ever?'

Well no, one is never 'crystallized', there is always something higher to reach for. Do you know the old statement—'there is always room at the top of a ladder!' I have often referred to the ninth dimension—okay, let me give you a new target, the nine hundredth dimension. Now, there is no point at all in trying to explain to you what the nine-hundredth dimension is, but there is a nine-hundredth dimension, and there are some higher. But if you cannot even understand the fourth or the fifth dimension, how can you even begin to understand the nine hundredth?

One rises and rises and rises. Of course, if one fights every inch of the way one is slower to rise, but people always have their opportunities, and I state definitely, definitely that no one is ever destroyed, not even the press people. Hey—you think I am going on about the press people? I have reason to, you know. I have had a lot of trouble with the press people in England and in Germany, in France and, as you will read later, in French-Canada too. But no, I am not bitter against the Press, I am not bitter against anyone. But it is stupid to sit down like Ferdinand the Bull and just smell the flowers while some ill-disposed people are trying to cut off one's tail for oxtail soup. Oh no, do not think that I am bitter, because I am not. Do not think that I am attacking the Press unfairly. I am not. I am telling the truth, *they* are the ones who cook up the tales!

But back to our dimensions; old Hitler, or Stalin, or a few others of that type, well they will not be bumped back to the first dimension, you know. They won't even get bumped back to the second dimension. They will come back to the third. And let me whisper something. Is your ear ready for a nice juicy whisper? Here it is then.

It is a fact that the real villain and tyrant of *this* life comes back to a new life as a ranting preacher. For instance, a man who has been a real sex pervert in one life may come ranting and preaching against sex in any shape or form, without having any regard as to how the race is to be continued. In the same way a fellow who was the chief torturer of a very fierce country will come back as a very, very sympathetic doctor, maybe. Things have to be equalized, you see. It is a case of lose one, gain one. You have to balance things out. So if you are a real thug in one life you come back as an imitation saint in the next because when you go to the Hall of Memories you see what a mess you made of things, so you return full of bitter remorse thinking what a scoundrel you were, and you go overboard rather, you overdo things, you become extreme, and so you get a real hearty old sinner coming back as one of these galloping priests who roar around the world teaching people to do nothing except squat on their haunches and bellow out a hymn or two. So—if you get any really good preacher in the next few years—well, it might just be old Hitler come back!

Now, how did I get into a bunch of questions like this? What am I having to work out by having myself saddled with such queries? Look at this one:

'Is all Creation composed of the vibrations of the musical octave with most of these octaves higher, or perhaps even lower, than human ears can detect?'

Everything is vibration, every single thing, even so-called dead matter vibrates, otherwise it could not exist. You get a lump of rock and you can't hear the noise it makes, but some creatures somewhere could, and they perhaps call the rock the singing stones or something, which would be a change from the Rolling Stones, wouldn't it? But all vibration is life, all life is vibration, and humans can perceive only the very minutest spectrum of vibrations. There are some places where rocks sing, and there are some places where rocks are, in fact, creatures. They may take a hundred years or so to make any movement which would be perceptible to humans, but these creatures, having a few millions of years of life according to Earth standards, are quite satisfied with their rate of movement. In any case they all go at the same rate so they don't know what slow pokes they are!

This next question logically, I suppose, should have been placed two questions higher. The question is: 'Is the Earth itself designed to evolve to a higher plane? Is the Moon on a plane below that of the Earth, and is this too destined to evolve to a higher plane and be replaced by another creation on the original level of the Moon's lower plane?'

Now my head is in a whirl with all that. How many questions is that in a bunch? I'd better stop for a moment until my head stops whirling!

Seriously though, the Earth is like a classroom. You wouldn't say that a classroom evolved, you wouldn't say the classroom of the Grade Three student suddenly evolves and becomes a Grade Four classroom or a Grade Five classroom. A classroom is a classroom and that's all there is to it. Of course many different collections of students pass through the classroom just as many different collections of civilizations pass through the Earth, and every so often there are tremendous cataclysms upon the Earth which plough up the surface of the planet so that all trace of life is lost and buried a few miles below the surface. That is why there is no trace of Mu or

54

Lemuria or Atlantis. That is why there are no traces of civilizations aeons before Atlantis itself.

Think of the farmer; he goes along with some horrible looking implement and all the surface of the field is churned up and turned over and ploughed deep so that there is a new surface ready for the fresh seeding. That is how the Earth is, that is how the Gardeners of the Earth go on. When a race gets too bad, along comes Something to turn over the surface of the earth and to bury all that which appertained to a previous decadent civilization, and then there is fresh earth upon which to plant fresh specimens.

The Moon, or the Moons, as the case may be, are not in any way inferior to the so-called parent planet. The Moon, in fact, may just be a large asteroid which has been caught by the gravitational field of that world which is about to become the predominant body, such as the Earth has the Moon as its satellite. And then you must also remember that people are used to life on Earth, they consider that all life must be that which is acceptable to them. It doesn't mean at all that life on the Moon (for example) must be identical to that upon the Earth. The people could, for instance, live inside the Moon.

To reply to this question, then, one can only say, No, the Earth does not evolve to a higher plane. It is just a classroom for people who are evolving.

A sudden commotion. The old man looked up from his work in some exasperation. Letters were bad enough to answer without unwelcome interruption, but the Visitor came in sight. 'Hi,' he said exuberantly, then sobered up a bit. 'Say, you never read the French language papers, do you?' 'No,' said the old man, 'I never read them at all, never even glance at them.'

'Well, you should, you know,' said the Visitor, 'they've been running quite a lot about you lately. Dunno what's biting them, I'm sure, but they seem to regard you as a personal enemy. What's the matter, wouldn't you give 'em an interview, or something?'

'No,' said the old man, 'I do not propose to give interviews to the Press because on every single occasion when I have given an interview my remarks have been grossly distorted in their reports. So it's better not to see any pressman and then

55

we know that any "interview" is entirely imaginary.'

The Visitor plucked at the lobe of his ear. 'Well, I dunno about that, because how are you going to tell people that you didn't give an interview after all? And even if you tell 'em, knowing how people are nowadays, they probably wouldn't believe it.'

'No,' replied the old man, 'this is one of the cases when you can't be right whatever you do.'

'Tell you something,' said the Visitor, 'I used to think you were a bit paranoid about the Press but some of the things I've seen lately and some of the things I've read lately lead me to believe that you're not such a nut after all. Seems everyone's had trouble with the Press. Listen to this.'

He ruffled about in his pockets turning out bales of paper and sorting through the tattered mass he came to a sheet which seemed to satisfy his search, so carefully he unfolded it and read: 'Now here's something for you. It's something that Thomas Jefferson said some years ago. He said—"Even the least informed of the people have learned that nothing in a newspaper is to be believed"—Now, what do you think of that? Now here's one, a real gem; Winston Churchill once wrote, "The essence of American journalism is vulgarity divested of truth. Their best papers write for a class of snotty housemaids and footmen, and even the nicest people have so much vitiated their taste as to appreciate this style." '

The old man smiled and said, 'Oh, I can do better than that, or if not better—as well. You know General William Sherman, a big American general, well, he once wrote, "I would rather be governed by Jefferson Davis than be abused by a set of dirty newspaper scribblers who have the impudence of Satan. They come into camp, poke about among the lazy shirks, and pick up camp rumours and publish them as facts, and the avidity with which these rumours are swallowed by the public makes even some of our officers bow to them as spies which, in truth, they are." '

But there was no point in going on on such lines so the old man said, 'Well, I've got work to do. You'll have to make tracks elsewhere for the time. I must get on with this or people will think I am a very bad author, that I can't reply to letters.

Beat it, will you?'

With a sigh and a hunch of the shoulders the old man turned back to his work again.

Now here is a question which should be of interest to many. It is: 'When I go to the Hall of Memories, if I decide I have learned what I set out to learn on this Earth do I move on to a plane of existence in a spirit world or do I take the human form again but live on a different planet in a different Universe?'

Well, if when you get to the Hall of Memories you decide that you have accomplished that which you set out to do, then you will not return to the Earth. There would be no point in so doing because you will have 'passed'. Think of school life again. Think if you go to a University or to a school, then there is no point in returning to cover a Course for which you already have a diploma. If you succeeded, and if you are satisfied that you have succeeded, then you can remain in the astral plane for an indefinite time or you can go on to another form of world where possibly the carbon molecule is not the basic brick of life, but maybe there is a silicone molecule or some other type of material. And there you could learn by kindness instead of by the hardship you endure on this Earth. There is hardship on this Earth because this is one of the hells. Cheer up, this hell will not endure for ever.

The same person asks: 'On the next plane of existence is the routine similar to that of the Earth, suffering, pain, and hardship until we have learned more lessons so that we may progress to the next plane of existence?'

Actually I have answered this quite a number of times, but let's go back to it again; Basically no, as you evolve higher and higher you have less and less to endure. Take as an example conditions on this Earth where the labourer gets the hard work, the bruises, and the bad language, etc., whereas the president or general manager of the company seems to make most of the profit, or at least that was so before the labour movement got under way and sort of reversed things—to the detriment of the world. But anyway, the point is that the higher you go the more rapidly you will progress and the easier are the conditions.

Mind you, I am actually referring to the basic physical things. No one will disagree that the labourer, digging holes in the ground, has quite a lot of physical hard work, he gets messy conditions, he gets the 'rough side of the tongue' from his foreman if he doesn't do his work properly. So he gets hard physical work.

But—the president of a company or the general manager may sit in comfort in a padded chair, but he does have a lot of 'non-physical' work to do. His is the responsibility for seeing that the less evolved (the labourers) are doing their work. So I do want to make it absolutely clear that the higher one goes the greater are one's moral responsibilities.

Look at it this way; the lowest labourers can go out and get drunk and have a fight and no one thinks anything about it, but if you got the higher people—a duke or a prince—if they went out on a pub-crawl and got involved in a fight, well, that just wouldn't do. And anyway, it wouldn't happen because as they progress upwards they get increased moral responsibility, increased moral and ethical discipline. They get greater respect in themselves and in their abilities, but the physical work is for the lower people, so that, when you are on this Earth, if you are in the lower stages, you have the hard work. When you progress upwards to other dimensions you do not have such hard and unpleasant conditions but, of course, you have greater responsibilities for which your hard work will have trained you.

Well, this person seems to be getting his money's worth; he's got a whole list of questions, but they are questions which seem to puzzle a lot of people. So here is his next question: 'What is the end going to be of all these planets that people live on, all these planes of existence? When the time comes that everybody has been through all the planes of existence and gained all the knowledge from these numerous lives, what do we do then?'

You cannot discuss this at present because of the limitations of the human three-dimensional comprehension. If you go into the astral world consciously you will know precisely what happens, and in terms of Earth or even human comprehension there is no end to it, it is like left-over meals; you start off with a good meal one day, the next day you get the thing hotted up, the day after that they make it into rissoles or something, and eventually it returns to the Earth, makes fresh plants which feed fresh humans, and so it goes on. It is an endless cycle of existence.

'You've told us in your books,' the questioner continues, 'that there are many Universes. Does our Universe overlap with any other or are there just voids of darkness between?'

There are billions and trillions of Universes. Now how can I make that clear to you? Well, let us imagine that you are on a seashore. At your feet there are all the grains of sand and these are in touch with each other, but you would not say that they overlapped, would you? Some are so small that they are dust, and some are great rocks, or even mountains, and, in fact, there are mountains beneath the sea just as there is sand beneath the sea. Think of all the grains of sand and all the rocks upon the Earth, but all the grains of sand upon the Earth, and all the rocks and all the stones upon the Earth do not in any way equal the number of Universes there are in the whole general system. And beyond this system there are others, on and on and on, *ad infinitum*, until we reach numbers far beyond human comprehension.

Still with the same gentleman. I have to answer this gentleman because up to the present I have done so many questions for the ladies that I do really welcome a gentleman with some sensible questions. But, anyway, he goes on: 'In one of your books you describe how you went astral travelling with your Guide, the Lama Mingyar Dondup and someone called Jigme to a Red Planet. When you were there you talked to some other people there who told you it was a dying planet. Were those other people in the astral form or in the human form, or did you materialize in front of them?'

You mustn't become confused between what is astral travel and what is physical travel. I didn't take a Greyhound bus to the Red Planet, that's for sure. But when one goes astral travelling one can still be completely visible *to a clairvoyant*, or completely audible *to a telepath*. So the Red Planet to which I went was populated, although extremely sparsely, and the population consisted of very highly evolved people who were clairvoyant and telepathic just as on this Earth people hear things and they see things. So they could actually see us just as if we were solid lumps of flesh and bones. They could talk to us and we could talk to them. We could see everything on their planet and they could see us. Actually, it was astral travel, conscious astral travel, astral travel under full control, but that made no difference at all to them and it made no difference at all to us. We were 'there'.

Now, here is something for you to think about. You read this a few times, then scratch your head and think about it some more:

You may be out in the street and you may see in front of you a person walking about in a perfectly ordinary and natural manner but—are you sure he really is there? Are you sure he is not an astral traveller who is stimulating your sensory perceptions to an extent that you believe he is a solid figure, whereas actually he may be in the astral vibrating on a frequency which is compatible to you and so you are sure that you actually see him with your physical eyes. You can't go up and take a poke at a perfect stranger and say, 'Hey, you, are you there or is it something else I see?' But if you could, and if your poking finger went right through him, you would probably drop from the shock, wouldn't you?

Another little thought, oh a nice little thought, this; you know all that talk about people who come out of Flying Saucers, or, to be more respectful, U.F.O.'s? Have you ever thought that if these people who came out of such things were so frightfully alien that we couldn't believe them, then we wouldn't see them, would we? Think that over. If a thing is too different from what humans can believe, they won't beleive it, and, not believing it, they won't see it.

Yet another simple little thought; these people may be of a different vibration, a vibration which is in the band of invisibility so far as humans are concerned. They can see humans, but humans can't see them. You think that sounds crazy? All right, how about this; dogs can hear sounds which humans cannot, so are you going to say that the sounds which dogs can hear and humans cannot are not there? The dog can hear the sounds and also hear the sounds which humans hear. The dog can hear both, so why should we not have people from another world on such a different range of vibrations that humans cannot perceive them? You think about that and then see if you don't feel somebody looking over your shoulder!

He has two other questions here which have already been answered in a previous book of mine. He asks: 'Did Man evolve from the sea—into apes—into Man? And where do the different races come from, out of space? The Gardeners of the Universe?'

That's easy! All you have to do to get those answers is read *The Hermit*; the how's and why's and wherefore's are given clearly in that book.

CHAPTER FOUR

One-Who-Could-Have-Been-A-Friend chuntered along the concrete-carpeted corridor. Breath coming in short, sharp gasps, he propelled his rotund body around the stone pillars, to come to a stop before a door hidden in a dusky alcove. Panting, he stood a moment to regain his breath, then with a stubby finger, he stabbed at the bell push. Inside the apartment behind the door a bell clanged noisily.

Inside the apartment the old man rested upon his bed. Sunlight streamed down upon the harbour waters. Down by the children's wading pool fond mammas gazed protectively at the end product of their amatory efforts. On the branch of a nearby tree a bird stood and sang of the joys of nesting time. The day was warm, cheerful, without a cloud in the sky.

The bell clanged. The sound of the door being opened. Mutter of voices: 'Can I see him a moment. It is urgent?' The clatter of footsteps and One-Who bustled beamingly into sight around the corner. 'Have you read this?' he squeaked, brandishing a copy of a very sensational French-language weekly. 'All about you. Libellous. Scandalous. They are going to write a book about you. Why don't you *do* something about it?'

The light of the sun gave no more warmth. A chill came to the air and a darkness crept over all. No more was the day gladsome. From the crumpled paper came the sinister emanations of *hate*, the hate of jealous men. A hate that had continued throughout many years. The hatred from authors whose books were not selling so well. Hatred, jealousy, concentrated venom against one who spoke and wrote the *truth*!

One-Who fidgeted with his hat and looked as though he

were having second-thoughts about imparting his information. 'You don't like the Press at all, do you?' he queried. 'The French-language lot seems to be writing quite a bit about you. And on TV too. Last night a Book Critic held up your latest book and said that he could not even read the first page of the first chapter, then he launched into a bitter attack on you personally. I wondered how he could attack so much if he had not read the book.'

The old man sighed. 'Yes,' he replied, 'there is a certain very noisy minority who are trying to harm not merely me, but the special work which I am trying to do. But never mind what a critic says, he is just a person who lacks the brains to write his own book—and is jealous of anyone who does. They confuse vicious sarcasm for wit. Don't bother about *them*!'

'But there must be *something* in it,' said One-Who, 'or the Press would not keep on so. There is no smoke without fire!'

The old man snorted with indignation. 'Shows how little *you* know,' he said, 'or you would not make such stupid statements.'

For a time he lay upon his bed just thinking of the past, thinking of the events of a decade and a half ago. In those days he had been living in London, England, and since the publication of the first book there had been difficulties. An Agency in Switzerland had put a wholly misleading advertisement in *The Times* reading, 'If Lobsang Rampa will communicate with —— he will hear something to his advantage.' So Lobsang Rampa, scenting a trap by intuition, got an Agent who was then Mr. Brooks of A. M. Heath & Company, to get in touch with the advertiser to see what it was all about. It was very informative. The Agency admitted they were doing wrong but said they had instructions from an author in Germany to find out all.

During those days the old man had been followed about, spied upon, and his life had been made a misery. During those days Buttercup came to live with him and Mrs. Rampa, came to live as an adopted daughter. Later she was to come to Canada as an adopted daughter. But prurient-minded people immediately saw sexual perversions in such an arrangement, perversions which in actuality did not exist. The young lady was accepted as a full member of the family, as an adopted daughter, but of course people with filthy minds could not accept such a statement.

The family left England, the land of persecution, and went to Ireland to the beautiful little village of Howth, near Dublin. There they made some very good friends indeed and still have those very good friends. But spurred on by a lot of lies the Press mounted a campaign of hatred and incorrect statements against Lobsang Rampa, saying all sorts of things, all sorts of untrue things. The stories they invented were far more miraculous than the absolute truth which Lobsang Rampa told.

One day a whole horde of beastly-minded British reporters descended upon the formerly peaceful village of Howth. They shattered the peace, they upset everyone, and one reporter in particular stole a garbage bin outside the Rampa house, ransacking it for anything he could find, and then threw it in someone else's garden, complete with all the garbage.

Fantastic, ferocious articles appeared in the English Press and in the German Press which was acting in close collusion with the English reporters. Lobsang Rampa was not able to do anything about the matter because he was ill in bed with severe coronary thrombosis. It was thought he would not live, but the Press seemed to hope that he would not live because that would have added to the sensation.

Pressmen came to the house. They yammered at the door like mindless creatures seeking only that which was evil, and not finding it, invented it. Mrs. Rampa was told they didn't want the truth. She was told that they wanted only sensation. The reporter-in-chief swore that he would stop the publication of any other book by Lobsang Rampa—this is the fourteenth! —and he seemed to be beside himself with insensate fury. The whole point of the matter was, though, that because of illness, because of extreme illness almost to the point of death, Lobsang Rampa could not bring a law case for libel. And because that opportunity has been lost the Press of the world now seem able to quote whatever they like from the original articles published in England and in Germany. Apparently, because no case was made within a certain time, it cannot be made now.

The British Press were filthy. The German Press were full

of outraged indignation. But why? They worked themselves into insane fury without cause because *The Rampa Story* is perfectly true, and the whole family has without any exception whatever affirmed that the whole thing is true. Lobsang Rampa is who he claims to be. One particular reporter printed a report saying that Mrs. Rampa had 'confessed'. It is not so. She had nothing to confess!

The story is true. Lobsang Rampa is all that he has claimed to be. He can do all the things he writes about. But because through illness he could not go to Court and defend his reputation, now the Press, like insensate morons, copy the original false articles and add to them out of a perfervid imagination. The French-language newspapers seem to derive a high delight out of what they imagine was the sexual aspect of it, quite oblivious of the fact that there was no sex connected with the affair. It was all a completely innocent, completely 'pure' association between two women and one man who lived as a hermit.

The old man thought of all these things. He thought of the difficulties which had been made not merely for him but for those who would come after, those who also would try to help this troubled world. He thought of the time of another press attack——

Lobsang Rampa was living in Windsor, Ontario, Canada. Unknown to him, in California, U.S.A., a man was claiming to be T. Lobsang Rampa, he was trying to collect 'disciples' and he was encouraging them to take mescalin and payote, saying it was good for their psychic development, etc., etc., and that Lobsang Rampa, without any exception whatever, has said that drug taking is absolutely harmless.

But Lobsang Rampa was in Windsor, Ontario, and the false Rampa was in Los Angeles. Inevitably the Los Angeles fraud was reported in the Press, and there was a great commotion about it. Eventually it was proved that Lobsang Rampa was not in California and the uproar died down, but the Press did not at any time publish an apology or state that a mistake had occurred.

The old man turned over on his bed and rustled some papers. Quite by chance he came up with three or four letters.

Glancing at them his thoughts ran on——

Two or three months ago letters began to come in, 'Where are my books? Where are the books you promised me?' A mystified Lobsang Rampa couldn't make head or tail of it until eventually there came a letter from Colorado saying that in the high part of Colorado there was a man living in a cave announcing publicly that he was T. Lobsang Rampa. He was telling people to drink intoxicating liquors and take whatever drugs they fancied. It was good, he said. He also advised people to write to 'Headquarters' and they would be sent a free set of the Rampa books. Hence the mail which descended on Lobsang Rampa, then living in Montreal.

An aroused Lobsang Rampa got in touch with the police in Colorado and applied quite a bit of pressure to the Chief of Police, pointing out what a bad advertisement it was for American justice if frauds could continue like this. So again another impostor was stopped.

There have been many such cases. The old man thought of the time when he had had letters from airline hostesses thanking him for the promise of the books, and asking where they were. Further letters produced the information that an impostor had been aboard the plane on their flight and had made quite a lot of ostentatious publicity. The fellow had said that he was Lobsang Rampa. He was going about with a lot of flair, a lot of bounce, saying how wonderful he was, promising free books for all. But not coming up with the books. And then hostesses and others writing in revealed the whole trickery. The Press never take such things into consideration. They never consider that people, like a horde of midges, persecute those of whom they are jealous. And so it is that the Press actually help those who are evil. The Press, it seems, will only give publicity to bad and never to good. They do nothing to correct a wrong. It seems—the old man thought—that in my case they have really gone overboard with their hatred, with their bias, they have quoted from my books, they have quoted from articles attacking me, and when complaint has been made they said, 'Oh, it's in the public domain, there is nothing you can do about it. We are within our rights.'

The television stations have been just as bad. There was, for example, a call some time ago from a television station. They issued an invitation. 'Come on television,' they said, 'tell us the story. Tell us the truth behind the Rampa Story.' So I was going to, I was going to say, Yes, the story is true, the Rampa Story itself is true; it tells the whole story, nothing more and nothing less. But they would not let me give my story. They insisted that instead I should read a prepared script, and that I refused because they wanted me to say I was a fake. But I am not. I am genuine. And that is why I could not appear on television.

There have been other cases like it. I have been given absolutely wonderful guarantees that I could write or say whatever I liked—'Put your own story over,' they said. 'Come on TV and say what you like. We won't stop you.' But as soon as an offer is taken up—no, they don't want the truth, they want only that which is sensational, only that which is untrue, only that which panders to the worst emotions of mankind. Hence, throughout these books, I have attempted to get at least one message over, and one message in particular is—All that I have written is true. My books are true, they contain my own experiences.

But One-Who was puttering around, fiddling with his feet, twiddling with his fingers. 'You ought to do an article yourself, you know,' he said. 'Why not tell the Press your side of the story? You know a man who is connected with the Press, why don't you call in Mr. Telly? He'd be glad to publish just as you tell your story. Sure, I can make the arrangement for you! I know him well. He'll come along, you'll find he is easy to get along with. Will you do that?'

The old man thought about it. He thought about the article in the crummy French-language newspaper, and then, reaching a sudden decision, he said, 'Yes! Tell the fellow to trot out his questions. Bring him along here, I'll give him an earful!!'

So One-Who smiled benignly, turned on his heel, and trotted out. The family came in, took one look at the old man's glum face, and said, 'Oh dear. More trouble? Is there never any end to it?'

But what *is* truth? What is your conception of truth? Do you know truth when you see it? How would you assess the truth of a statement? Would you prefer to accept the word of a person who can demonstrate truth, or would you prefer to accept the word of people like press reporters who just want something which is sensational? But, of course, not only the press people are at fault. The public are at fault also because just within the past few weeks I have heard of an absolutely authentic case of a man in the U.S.A. This man had what he believed to be the right idea. He wanted to bring good to the people so he started a newspaper devoted to good, devoted to the better aspects of the daily news, and now the paper has closed down. People do not want to hear good news, they only want to hear bad news. People do not want to hear how well a person has done, but they are interested only in the bad things.

Many people are now trying to 'pull down' Churchill and others of that immense stature because it makes them feel 'great' to find out something about Churchill—it doesn't matter if it is something true or false, if it is repeated enough, people will believe it. But let me tell you what I think about truth.

In this day and age when fourteen-year-olds complain that they cannot 'communicate' with even sixteen-year-olds, we must define our terms so that the reader can understand what the writer is trying to say. *What-is-truth?* Truth, as I see it, is a statement of *facts*, things which have occurred, things which *are*, things which are not the figments of an imagination but the quality or state of being in accordance with experience, in accordance with that which actually occurred. *That* is truth.

Precisely! That describes my books exactly; 'The quality of being in accordance with experience.' I—experienced—*all*—that—which—is—written—in—my—books, wherefore it is that I write *truth*.

Imagination, conversely, is the act or power of creating mental images of that which has never been actually experienced. *My* powers of cerebration are not those which would enable me to write fiction; my astrological make-up absolutely inhibits such a display of cerebral virtuosity—wherefore it is that I am *compelled* to write only the truth.

Let me repeat myself a little, even at the risk of some ill-natured person writing to say, 'You told us all that before.'

People do write in such a manner, you know. So many people are wholly unable to understand the viewpoint of others. They have never had any experience themselves and so they just like to be vicious and—as I said before—pull everyone down to their own miserable level.

Every so often there is a silly season in the Press; there is not much news about, a war has ended, or the latest sex symbol has got married or has died or something else, and so bored reporters react to bored editors made irate by idleness by hatching up some 'scandal' which really does not exist in fact. Sometimes some poor wretched schoolteacher is accused of a heinous crime and is pilloried on hearsay evidence for something of which he is quite innocent.

Having been framed, accused, judged, and condemned by the vicious Press of England and Germany with papers in other countries copying, I am going to give some details about it because, as you will have read in the foregoing pages, the Press is *still* attempting to 'execute' me as they have attempted unceasingly during the past fifteen years.

In my innocence I thought that every person accused of something had the right to be confronted by his accuser, I thought that every person had the right to defend himself, but—and I say this to you very seriously—the Press have without exception refused to allow me to give my side of the story. They have refused to allow me any opportunity of defending myself. It is like some big bully with a high-powered public address system trying to shout down a person who can only whisper. Okay, I am whispering to you. Will you listen?

I am an author who really had no intention of becoming one. In England many years ago I tried without any success at all to obtain employment. I was too old or too 'different', or too this or too that. I went (as you can read in my books) to Employment Agencies and to all manner of strange places, all without success. Then I was given a personal introduction to see an Authors' Agent who, it was said, might have 'something useful'. Well, the Agent, no doubt with an eye to profitable business, refused to give me a job, saying, 'I've heard about you; write a book about your own life.'

I left his office in disgust and, I admit, with considerable anger because once again I had been brought on a fool's errand. Nothing was further from my mind than book writing. I thought that it was such a silly sort of thing. Unemployment and the hunger which it caused prevailed, and eventually with extreme reluctance I wrote a *true* book about my life, a *true* book! I bared a past which I very much wanted to conceal, I bared it and wrote about it so that I could eat.

But there was jealousy; the fact that I was a success aroused the ire of certain people with much money and—to put it bluntly—I was 'framed' and attacked when through serious illness I was quite unable to defend myself.

No one has ever been able to *prove* me a fraud; for every 'expert' who claimed that I was such—three or more attested to my complete genuineness. I was never accused before a Court of Law, instead there have been only the sickening innuendos of the Press and others, innuendos which I could not refute at the time because of coronary thrombosis.

The Press, the television stations, and the radio have consistently refused to give my side of the story. They have refused to print or transmit my statement that all my books are absolutely true. Instead they keep on hatching up a rehash of the whole affair, adding lies to lies until in the end one just does not know what is what.

I am reminded of the person of whom I have just told you, the man who started a good newspaper and whose venture failed because people like scandal, people like doing harm to others. The Press know that if I should prove myself absolutely true then it would not help their circulation. Only scandal, murder, rape, etc., is a useful commodity to the Press.

People *like* to say, 'Oh yes, I know it's true, I read it in the Press.' It's a case of give a dog a bad name and hang him before he can say anything in his defence. In my case this attitude really has caused much harm. I had hopes of being able to help Tibet by speaking before the United Nations, and, in fact, I claim that my books have helped Tibet and the cause of Tibet enormously because my remarks have made the country known, my remarks have made the 'strange' people 'human'.

Yet, in spite of the help I could give, some of the exiled 'high officials' in India have said unkind things about me because, I understand from a reputable source, they have been told to discredit me or lose the help given by certain religious organizations. It may be asked how can these spiritual Leaders (so-called) discard one of their own? But Chairman Mao and General Chiang Kai Shek are both Chinese, both try to discredit the other. Even here in Canada where I now live, Mr. Stanfield tries his utmost to discredit Mr. Trudeau, or old Tommy Douglas chips in and tries to discredit everyone. It seems to be an occupational hazard.

But let us look at another case; in Northern Ireland Christians kill each other because two sorts of Christians each think that only they are right, both sides are Irish, both sides are Christians, both sides appear to believe in the same things, yet they fight and kill each other, and the Press by inflammatory reporting add fuel to the flames. If 'good Christians' behave like this is it not understandable that Tibetans in India, under considerable political and religious pressure, may 'under orders' repudiate one of their own elsewhere 'for the great good of the majority'?

My books are true. Yes, but people lose the whole point of the matter. It does not matter if I was born in Lhasa or Londonderry; the author does not matter, what the author writes, does. Have these books helped you? Have they helped anyone? Has anything been learned from them? Yes? Then they are worth while. You, the reader, pay a few cents or a few pence for a paperback book. That minute sum does not automatically entitle you to set up as a prosecutor, jury, judge, and executioner, yet that is what some of you are trying to do and actually loving it.

But there it is. It is your choice what you believe. I say my books are true. Now I do not claim that idly, I claim it because thousands of people have written to me and told me that my books have helped them, have stopped them from committing suicide, have helped relatives who were dying, have removed fear of death, etc., etc. Do you not think that in view of all this I am entitled to a little consideration, to a little politeness instead of the ranting Press always hanging around my doors? As you will read later they eventually drove me away from Montreal.

71

I am going to quote from *The Gazette of Montreal* for Thursday, June 15, 1972. The headline is 'Tibetans in Quebec are Trying Hard to Keep Tradition Alive. Strangers in a Promised Land.'

' "We are going to be strangers for a long time," Lynne Borjee murmured softly over the top of her teacup.

'She glanced quickly at her friend, Kesang Ichhemorito, and smiled wistfully as she hunted for the right English expression.

'——Kesang at 22 is a shy, reticent girl with high cheekbones and an infectious grin, but she admits to a distrust of Montreal newspapers.

' "When we first came here a French paper wrote a story about us which said that we didn't even know what a swimming suit was and that we went swimming in our raincoats. We may be from another country but we are not stupid." The story did not please Lynne much either, "WE NEVER EVEN SAW THE REPORTER WHO WROTE THE STORY," she said.'

Where is the truth in that? The Press reporter or the Tibetan refugees?

Yes, I certainly get to know all manner of strange things. For example, our old friend Mr. John Henderson, of whom you have heard in the past, sent me a cutting and apparently I cannot quote much from it because—well, because my publisher thinks I should possibly be infringing someone's copyright, and one has to please a publisher, hasn't one? Anyway, Mr. Henderson sent me a cutting from the *Charlotte Observer* dated August 26, 1971, and the headlines are startling enough: 'Japanese Say Jesus Died, Buried There At Age 112.' The headlines go on: 'Jesus Not Crucified—Documents. Japanese Claim Christ Sacrificed Brother On The Cross Then Fled.' The article is by John Justin Smith. Apparently the fellow is a reporter on the *Charlotte Observer* staff, but it would be quite interesting for some of you who live in the U.S.A. to get hold of that paper and read all the details which are given there. They are very circumstantial details—very authentic reading.

I have a very close friend in Japan and this young lady to whom this book is dedicated made some enquiries for me, and —well, I strongly advise you to get hold of that newspaper

because some of you will find it really interesting. E
to remember the exhortation and injunctions of Mr. I
(bless his soul!), and so the best thing we can do n
answer some more questions. I have some very good on

Yes, that's right too, some of these questions *are* quite good.
For example, 'Please can you explain how Art or other creat-
ive activities increase one's vibrations? And how beneficial are
such vibrations?'

Actually everyone and everything, as I have told you before,
consists of vibrations. There are negative vibrations and there
are positive vibrations, and I do not know how many of you
have ever played with tuning forks. But if you have two tuning
forks you can hold one with its end on a table, and then you
could bang on the other tuning fork to set it humming, and
place that with its end on the table quite a distance away from
the first tuning fork—and the first tuning fork would start
humming in sympathy with the other. Get hold of a pair of
tuning forks from your music store, they are cheap enough, try
it and you'll find it is really quite interesting.

When we get vibrations which are pleasant it makes us
vibrate more pleasantly, that is, it increases our rate of vibration and thus makes us happier, more spiritual, more percep-
tive. But if we get a thing which depresses our vibrations then
we get nasty-minded, lower spiritually, and it definitely stops
spiritual progress.

Painting, after all, is just a set of materials arranged in such
a fashion that the entire vibration is such that it pleases us and
increases our rate of vibration. So Art, whether it be a picture
or music, can increase our spirituality by raising our vibration.
Remember, high vibrations are good and positive, low vibrations are negative and not always so good.

The next question is a good one, and it really does fit in
with the question above. A lady writes: 'This is a question so
many people would, I believe, like some information on—fear.
You have described how fear is nothing more than uncontrolled imagination struggling with will-power and that will-
power will always fail in the struggle. What is the cause of
fear?'

Let's go back to Art; if we see something beautiful we ap-

73

reciate it, we like it, we get pleasure from it. But if we see something terrible—what shall I say? A picture of devilish tortures?—whatever it may be, if it is a terrible, beastly, horrible thing it depresses our vibrations and we get to thinking, 'Oh, suppose that should happen to me!' Then immediately it sets up a chain reaction in our vibrationary make-up and the unpleasant vibration which we call fear feeds upon itself and produces more fear.

You get the same thing sometimes when people pass a graveyard at midnight and something stirs. The hair on the back of their necks sticks up and there is a great temptation to start off at a run because the imagination lowers the vibrations so that one is susceptible to impressions from the lower astral of disembodied spirits, bodies in coffins and all the rest of it, and we think that such things could happen to us, we think that a ghost is going to come out and bite us behind, or something. Well, we think about that and we fail to be rational about it, and so the fear grows and grows. In other words, the vibrations become lower and lower and we become gloomier and gloomier.

Fear is nothing but uncontrolled imagination. If you want to overcome fear just *be certain* that nothing is going to hurt you. Nothing can hurt you. Tell yourself that you are an immortal soul and although it is possible for someone to temporarily damage your clothes or your body that will not hurt the essential *you*. The less you fear fear the less you will have fear, so that in the end you can discipline yourself so much that fear does not exist, cannot exist, in your make-up. Then you will know contentment and satisfaction, then you will walk with your head up and your shoulders back (unless you live in a wheelchair!).

Now, listen to this—'You have described how drugs can do great harm to one's spirituality. Can such damage be repaired within a lifetime? You say, also, that one should never take drugs, but surely you will agree that many people have secured out-of-the-body experiences by the use of drugs, have secured spiritual enlightenment through the use of drugs. I believe you are wrong when you say that drugs are harmful. What do you say about that?'

Yes, ma'am, I do say that drugs are wrong. I do say that drugs are the work of the devil himself because if you take drugs then you are altering your vibrations artificially and you are making it almost impossible (I said 'almost') to develop spiritually without the aid of such props.

Drugs are terrible things indeed and they definitely stain your astral body and impair your physical body.

Do you believe that athletes should be given drugs to make them run faster or jump higher? Do you believe that people should take Benzedrine tablets to keep them going longer? If you do you should read some of the police reports. For an illustration I will tell you about long-distance truck drivers; these men drive vast distances every day and, naturally, they get tired. So many of them have been in the habit of taking drugs or, as they term them, 'goof-balls', and police records and insurance statistics quite irrefutably prove that the use of these drugs causes accidents, death, and mental impairment. Now if drug firms could do so with safety they would sell all manner of drugs, they are in the business to make money, but it is stupid to go on selling stuff like LSD, goof-balls, and the like, and then find that they are injuring the health of so many people. I say that drugs should be quite definitely banned.

But those who have taken drugs, what hope have they? They have every hope provided they most rigidly abstain from taking drugs any more, provided they eat sensibly and drink sensibly, and provided they do not go in for too many forms of abuse—self-abuse, that is. No one is 'beyond the pale'. Everyone can be helped if they want to be helped. So if any of you who are drug addicts really want to 'kick the habit', then you can 'kick the habit' and by the time you get to the Other Side you will find that your astral form has recovered from the psychic shock of your physical drug addiction.

I do want to say something here about suicide because of late I have been shocked at the number of people who have written to me saying that they have been on drugs and they see no way out except to commit suicide. Well, my goodness me! Suicide is very very wrong indeed. You harm yourself, and you have to come back to much worse conditions if you commit suicide. If you have difficulties which make you think about suicide, then talk over the matter with a priest, or even with the Salvation Army, or look in the telephone directory and find some Association or Society connected with Welfare with whom you can discuss your problems. So let me emphasize as I have emphasized so often in the past—*never contemplate suicide. Never commit suicide.* You are hurting yourself if you do. If you commit suicide, well, you have abandoned help. If you stay alive there is always some way out of your problem. Suicide is not a way out because—I repeat—you come back to harder conditions.

Now another question: 'How is it that some people come to one sign of the Zodiac and some to another sign? If we come as a Taurus person how can we appreciate the problems of a Cancer person or a Leo person or a Scorpio person, or something else? I don't understand this problem about how we come under different signs of the Zodiac. Will you tell us?'

Yes, I can tell you. Every person goes through every sign of the Zodiac, and there are twelve signs. And every person has to live through each quadrant of the Zodiac. So you can be just entering the sign of Libra in one life, then in another life (not necessarily the next) you can be right midway in the sign of Libra, and in yet another life you can be just leaving the sign of Libra, or, of course, all the other signs of the Zodiac. So you have to live through every sign and every part of the sign so that you get full experience of each of the signs.

Question: 'Tell us about the future. Are we in the West all going to be "in for it", or will things suddenly brighten for us? Tell us, will you? I've just bought a place up in the Rockies in Washington State, I am having a house built there, and I am hoping to be free of all troubles. Will I be?'

Well, we have to remember that everything comes in cycles. Imagine that you are watching a great big pendulum. The pendulum is at the top of its stroke. Let us say you are facing this pendulum and it is up at the top of its stroke on the right-hand side. Then you release it, and it moves down and eventually it reaches its lowest point, and then it rises to go up to its highest point. Then it reverses and comes down to the lowest point, and up again. Life—existence—is like that. You get a Golden Age and then people are too self-satisfied so things get worse and worse, things get lower and lower just like the pendulum on its downward swing. And then, when it is nearly at the bottom of its swing, you get the negation of all liberties, you get Communism when people get horribly sick of being dictated to. After that they strive again for freedom and so, just as the pendulum moved to the upward stroke, people strive for more spirituality and they work hard at it, they put aside their petty bickering, they put aside their fighting, conditions improve. Eventually life becomes quite pleasant, then it becomes exceedingly good, better and better. And so we come again to a Golden Age, an Age in which people get complacent, too self-satisfied, too content. So they sit back, they've got everything, there is nothing more to work for. And then the pendulum starts on its downward swing again, and so people find hardship coming, they find Communism comes again, and so we get the same thing cycle after cycle.

Now upon this Earth we are having a hard time. The pendulum is still going down, and it has to go down still further before it can go higher, but cheer up—the Communism the world will know will not be so severe as that which initiated that evil cult or policy into this world because each time conditions get a little better. So—we are approaching the darkest hour before the dawn, but after the darkest hour shafts of light will shine across the sky, the gloom will end, the day will dawn, and again we shall come to the Golden Age. But at the end of the day the night will fall again, to be followed by gloom and darkness until again dawn will burst upon the world and life will become brighter and brighter until, with increasing complacency and self-satisfaction, conditions will deteriorate. And so until the end of Time the Earth and all worlds have these cycles of good and bad, and good and bad. So be of good cheer because no one is ever alone or deserted. There is always hope, so keep that in mind. You can be as good as you want to be. You can be helped at any time if you really want to be.

CHAPTER FIVE

It was becoming difficult to go out in the grounds or to drive along the Plaza in the wheelchair. Curtains would twitch slightly at my passing and perhaps just one eye would show as an inquisitive person followed my transit.

Whispers came: 'Yes, that's him all right—that's him.' Others, more forthright, came out in the open and said they had heard about me on French television or they had read about me in the French-language papers. Some went so far as to say that there seemed to be quite a conspiracy to do whatever harm they could.

The number of visitors who were 'just taking snapshots' increased. It was noticeable that they all managed to aim the camera in my direction. On one occasion I was riding along in my wheelchair by the side of the road and a car came rushing out of the distance and slowed up with a screech of brakes beside me. The driver drove along at my speed and—highly dangerously—he used a cine camera to film me at the same time as he was trying to drive his car on a public road!

There came the time when the whispers and the irritations became unsupportable, so we discussed matters and I said, 'Oh, let's get this Mr. Telly in then, but I will tell you what I am going to do; I have had so much double-crossing from people, not only the Press but from all manner of people, that I think I will use a tape recorder and record what is said so that afterwards, if there should be any dispute—well, then I shall have evidence to prove what happened free from defective memories, free from what I may gently call "reporters licence".'

Within a very few days there came a rush and a roar, something like a modern jet plane taking off or a space capsule or something, and the very fast modern car belonging to Mr. Telly swooshed up the road, violently turned right, and swung down to the entrance many floors below. Minutes later there came hurrying footsteps and almost a 'skid stop' followed by pounding at the door. Mr. Telly entered.

Of course it must be very clearly understood that 'Mr. Telly' is not his real name. His real name doesn't matter, it has nothing to do with this book, but I thought that as television and newspaper, radio and all that were much the same sort of racket I would invent a generic term. This must be made clear because in the past I have really, truly, honestly, seriously had people write to me and ask me about Mrs. Hensbaum and Rosie Hipps, and people like that, not realizing that I was just using made-up names.

Well, Mr. Telly came in. We had a few friendly words of greeting and then he told me that he'd got a whole list of questions, and I said, 'Well, look, I am a very sick man indeed and I do not know that I can stand all the time and hardship or many hours of interview, so what I suggest is this; you give me all your questions and I will answer some of them here and now and I will answer the others in writing.'

Mr. Telly nodded wisely and produced wads of paper from his pocket. Some had pretty doodles on them for he was a great doodler. And then he put the questions on the bed before him.

'Before we start,' I said, 'I do want you to understand clearly Mr. Telly that in this material I retain my copyright because I propose to use all this material in a book which I am going to write for the English language. You do understand that, don't you?'

Mr. Telly looked a bit sour, and said, 'Oh well, how am I going to manage then if it is your copyright? I cannot use the material myself, can I?'

'Well yes, you can, Mr. Telly,' I said, 'for I am telling you that you can use all this material in the French book which I understand you are going to write, and I will use it in the English book so then we shall not conflict with what we are going to do, shall we?'

Mrs. Rampa, who was listening intently, nodded sagely and then Mr. Telly said, 'Oh well, that's all right then.'

'Now then,' I said, 'this picture you brought from that French-language paper—well, it makes me rather sorry that I am not more proficient in French. It's interesting that these fellows label me as a "gentle fake". Actually I am neither gentle nor a fake, but surely their comments are some sort of a compliment because there is so little gentleness in the world today; it seems that Jews and Arabs are knocking the stuffing out of each other, and Christians are trying to see what is inside the other fellow, and bombs are being tossed about in Montreal, and the Press and Television are being savage to anyone. Yes, I suppose it is quite a compliment to be labelled "gentle" even if it is in the connotation of fake.

'But, you know, this just shows how inaccurate the Press really is because I have always maintained that it does not matter who writes a thing so long as the person writes stuff that is of benefit to other people, so long as he writes the truth. That is what I say, I say it does not matter about me, it does not matter who I am, it does not matter what I am. If what I write brings some good to someone—and letters which I have prove that I do bring good to people—then my precise identity, or whether I sign my name with an A, a Y, or a Z, surely does not matter. This interview, you know, is really just pandering to the inquisitiveness of the public. You seem to think that it is a good idea but I am not sure that I agree with you.

'One of the complaints I have is this; I tell the absolute truth and yet the Press wriggle around taking my statements out of context, and making up something quite different which I certainly did not say and did not imply. I state that all that I have written is true. How can anyone distort that? But I have no doubt that the Press will distort it somehow. Why do not the Press go in for some research? Surely they have enough money for it. They could do some research into authentic cases of transmigration. Even in the Bible there are cases of transmigration, and throughout history, throughout the Libraries of the world, there are many really authentic cases recorded (I must be careful when I say "really" authentic because otherwise some moronic pressman will say, "Oh, he uses 'really' therefore he is implying he is not genuine." But that is not so at all). I state that I have experienced definite, authentic trans-migration.

'Now you ask about this plumber business. Well, what is wrong with being a plumber? I am sure you have found the services of a plumber extremely useful at times, in fact at times the services of a plumber can be a darn sight more bene-ficial to you than the services of a pressman. You get locked in the smallest room, for instance, and it takes more than a press-man to get one out.

'However, whether you believe it or not (and I couldn't care less), no—I have never been a plumber. If I had I would be far richer than I am at present because I believe that plumbers are extremely well paid. Certainly they charge enough!

'I have just said about you being locked in the smallest room, but there is one report which I had repeated to me some time ago which gave me very considerable glee; there was a pressman with a very bad character—one who persecuted me without mercy—and he went aboard a ship to do some inter-viewing and he was not at all wanted, he was not popular even with his fellow reporters, and if anyone is unpopular with a fellow reporter then he must be a pretty crummy specimen indeed. But, anyway, this reporter had to go to the you-know-where, and while he was in that very small space some of his associates barricaded the door preventing him from coming out. Consequently he missed the interview altogether, and that was a good thing because he was not a good writer nor did he know the meaning of truth. But then, this could apply to all pressmen, couldn't it?

'Returning to this plumber business—no, I do not know anything about it because, as I have stated, my story is a true story and the pages in *The Rampa Story* will give you as much as I know about this past life. Look at it like this; you go to a cinema show and you see a film which, for some extraordinary reason is being run backwards, that is, the film runs from now to then. Well, you become confused, your sense of time is altered because everything is reversed. But you try to remem-ber a film you saw—oh, what shall we say?—twenty years

81

ago? How much do you know about it now? Probably you were not all that interested, and if you wrote out exactly what happened in that film which is being run backwards, it would not necessarily tally precisely with actual events. I have a completely eidetic memory about everything which has happened to *me*—to me personally. But I am not good at all at trying to portray the life story of a person whom I have never met and whom I never want to meet.

'What is transmigration? Well, I thought everybody knew what that was. If they don't know what it is then they can't be very good at their religious studies, can they?

'Transmigration is stated to be the movement of one soul from one body into another body. There are many, many recorded instances in the world's history in which the soul of a person has departed from a body but before death occurred to that body another body was taken over. It is as simple as that.

'You can say if you wish to make it clearer that there is a car. The car stops and the driver gets out. Another driver gets in and drives off. The driver, in this case, can be likened to the soul. So the soul, which is the first driver, left the car which is the body, and a fresh soul, which is the second driver, got into the car and drove off. Just as you can have a car which is driven by two people—one after the other of course—so you can have a body which is occupied first by one soul and then by another. There is nothing very strange about it.

'Another way in which you can look at it, if it helps to make it clearer, is this; you have a storage battery, and the charge, which in this case is the soul, goes out of it with use, so then it is charged up again and, in effect, the same battery gets a different soul.

'The difficulty is that here in this Western part of the world people are more interested in making money and in harming their neighbours, but in the Eastern part of the world there is a completely different concept of the purpose of living. In the Far East people are more interested in the spiritual side of life, things of the spirit have greater value than the things of the flesh.

'But you are still on about this plumber business and how it started. Well, in England there are many snobs, we must admit that, and if a person is a plumber or a garbage collector then he is considered to be pretty low and not to have any education, and is supposed to touch a greasy forelock and say, 'Yes, God, No, God,' to the customers who do not pay their bills. So the best way to pull a man down in England is to say, 'Oh, he's the son of a plumber,' or 'He is a plumber himself,' which, I gather, is considered to be even worse. I cannot help smiling, though, when I think that the Founder of the Christian Religion was a carpenter, which is no higher than being a plumber!

'I have been reminded of a case which illustrates this very well. Lord Hambledon is an important and cultured man but there was someone talking about him in a disparaging manner, and remarked, 'Oh that fellow Smith who sells books.' That, however, still does not affect the true status of Lord Hambledon whose name is also Smith and who is, after all, England's biggest and perhaps most important bookseller.

'This is the Age of Kali, the age of disruption where the crummy little man-in-the-street and his snotty-nosed wife, done up with loads of powder and face goo, try to pull down all that really matters, try to sneer at tradition, try to sneer at culture, and have no time for education because through television and the Press people are very superficially educated above their means and above their brains! They hear fantastic tales about Hollywood homes, and they get Communist ideas that they too should have such homes, homes which really exist only in the fevered imagination of the film people.

'The worst aspect of our present civilization is how a very noisy minority can make it appear that a person is a fraud or a person is hated, etc. We get the same thing in strikes. We get a few hooters rousing the general people to an absolute frenzy. We get strong-arm goons who beat a person senseless if he tries to stand on the side of decency. And so the average person who would like to know the truth is driven by fear to listen to the rabble and the goons and the Press.

'But you tell me something; if a man has a big firm, or if he supervises, does he necessarily have to be classed as the lowest of the lot? For instance, if a man owns a newspaper does he have to be just the copy-devil or whatever you call the fellow nowadays. Or if a man has a great big home appliance firm, does he count as a pipe-fitter or a plumber, or is he the head of the firm? It is a terrible thing nowadays how people are so unutterably snobbish. What was Moses? Surely Moses was a waif, a homeless child who was just picked up somewhere. And what was Jesus? The son of a carpenter, we are told. And here again, as I said previously, that is an even older trade than that of a plumber.

'To bring it back to our present era the Press have also started a good thing in their own mind by bringing down royalty. Do they not refer so frequently to Princess Margaret as "Mrs. Jones"? Do they not refer to that very great man, Prince Philip, as just a foreigner who managed to get adopted into the British Navy or something? Strange, isn't it? And so why should we not call the Editor of a newspaper a rag-picker? After all, he does have a rag, does he not?

'Again, I am going to state that all my books are true, and I am going to tell you that I have a very special reason for insisting on this truth. I will even tell you why I so insist; transmigration is fact, not fantasy, and there will be many others like me coming to this world. If I can save any of those from the misery and hell and persecution which I have endured through hatred here, then my own suffering will have been more than justified.

'People who have accomplished transmigration, and have talked about it, have been regarded as something strange. Some have been put in mental homes! But if a person appears strange to another person he is feared, and if he is feared he is also hated. Have you ever seen a dog approaching a strange dog? Have you seen how it circles around, sniffing and growling, and is always afraid it is going to lose something? Well, that is how humans behave with me because they consider that I am different in some way, and so they try to claim that I am a fraud, they try to claim that because I am so strange I must be a fake. I am not, you know. I am one alone at present—the lonely man—but there will be others coming by transmigration, and they will carry on where I have to leave off through ill health and poverty, both caused by persecution.

'People persecute and fear that which they do not understand. People hate those who take them into realms which they have not before entered. People loathe those who write about matters beyond the limited experiences of the reader. People try to destroy that which does not conform to their own concepts and patterns, as witness the assorted Christians in Northern Ireland trying to destroy all the other Christians whose concepts may be microscopically different. As witness the American Whites trying to enslave or destroy the American Coloureds because they do not conform to the white pattern. The path of the bringer of truth is hard; only the sadist and the pornographer is lauded and loaded with gold. No matter the consequences, all my books are true.

'My wife has been approached by pressmen who wanted her to write something sensational, something that the public could lap up. It did not have to be true. If it was the truth, so they said, it would not be sensational, it would be just—the truth. But one man offered her quite a considerable sum of money to deny everything that I claim and to make out all sorts of strange things. He wanted sex orgies, he wanted underground temples, and obscene rites. Naturally my wife refused. But it shows that there is a little segment of the Press out to falsify the truth. They cannot bear the truth, it has no interest for them.

'There has been an astonishing interest in my sex life! Now, I can answer that easily, that is very very simple to answer: I do not have a sex life, I live as a hermit. One could say (and it has been said too often), that I live as a lodger in my own home, but there is no trouble with morality here. Each of us has respect for the others, and, you know, we are not all sex mad perverts. We leave that for others.

'Oh yes, I must tell you this; this should make you laugh. I had one communication from a lady, a French-Canadian of course, who stated with great triumph that she knew I was a fake because I looked at my cats with love when she saw me on a filmed programme. Love my little cats? Of course I do! I really, genuinely love both these little people, I love all cats, but I do not always extend that love to humans.

'Now a word straight from the horse's mouth, or am I just a

85

donkey instead, for being lured into this? But anyway, here is a word straight from my mouth; it really astounds me how Press people drum up a lot of criticism when they have not even read my books. Now if somebody wants to criticize my books, and if they know something about the subject, why do they not read the books first? Probably because they will find that there is nothing they can criticize after. However, there it is. Yes, you can put all this into print if you want to, I would agree to it, but only if you include this sentence:

'I, T. Lobsang Rampa, state definitely that all my books are true and I am whom I claim to be, and I state that others will come by transmigration. I hope they will get a better welcome than I did.

'Oh, good gracious, I thought we had finished all these foolish questions. But if, as you say, it is so vitally important to answer them, what are they? Critics' queries? But, I don't mind critics! These people who criticize because they are ignorant and don't know anything. But come on, bring out your questions. What are they, and what is the first one?'

Q: 'People write in and say that you do not look like a Tibetan.'

A: 'Oh, they do, do they? But how many people of any nationality look as popular imagination would have them look? Take, for example, England, a small country. Can you say that anyone is a typical Englishman? Consider a small dark Welshman, compare him with a big blonde Scotsman. Do they look alike? They are both still people of Great Britain, aren't they? Then take a person from Manchester and a person from Cornwall, they are both English but they may be utterly, utterly different.

'Consider high-caste Indians. Some of them are so white-skinned that they can and do pass for Europeans. But the typical Indian of distorted imagination might be a small dark little man, usually clad in rags. That is nonsense. It is quite absurd to say that there is a classical person of any race. For example, John Bull, the typical British cartoon figure; is there such a person? Or Uncle Sam—is there such a person as Uncle Sam? No! People who say, "Oh, he doesn't look like a Tibetan," are just displaying their ignorance of life and life's forces. The average Tibetan of popular Western imagination is of Mongolian origin, but the higher the caste of Tibetan the whiter and the more "European" he appears to be.'

Q: 'What can you tell us about reincarnation? People write in and say that reincarnation is a thing they really cannot accept.'

A: 'What a fantastic thing that is! Reincarnation is or has been taught in most religions. For an illustration, let me remind you that the original teachings of Christ are very very different from the teachings of the present. Things are changing. Often the Vatican will issue an edict changing an interpretation; a person who has been a saint for centuries is no longer a saint. Dogma which has been accepted for centuries becomes changed overnight by papal edict.

'The same thing happens in the case of reincarnation. Christ taught reincarnation. He taught that people came back time after time and then went back to the place where "In my Father's house there are many mansions". But the priests round about the Year 60 decided to alter the teachings of Christ and they found that it was not wise to teach reincarnation because people would have a jolly good time in one life thinking they would pay for it in the next life, in the comfortable distant future. So in the Christian belief reincarnation was dropped. The original documents, the Dead Sea Scrolls and all that type of thing teach reincarnation. But isn't it amusing that I, a non-Christian, should have to teach the Christian belief to Christians?

'Many religions believe that people have to come to this Earth as children return to school time after time. Children first go to the infants' class, then at the end of that term they go home for recreation. At the end of the recreation they are "born" to the school life again. If they have done well enough in their previous term they come back to a higher grade. Then, when they have continued successfully for that term, they "die" to the school life and return home again, going back to school after the suitable holidays. So they go on like that, returning to school until the end of the school career. At the end of each successive term they return home, only to go back to school in a higher grade until they have progressed through the school, or, as we have to point out, life. Then they return home to come back to school no more, or come back to Earth no more.'

Q: 'I have here a French magazine. It prints the information that you are a plumber. It says that you have been a plumber all your life. What about that?'

A: 'So we get back to this plumber business again, eh? Well, I wish I could charge the going rate for plumbers. I could do quite well on that money. But no, I repeat, I am not a plumber, I have never been a plumber, and—well—how can they possibly say that I am now living as a plumber when actually I am either bed-ridden or confined to a wheelchair? That just shows how press reports are frightfully inaccurate.'

Q: 'People say that you are very rich, that you live in absolute luxury.'

A: 'Just look about you! Do you think this is luxury? Did you not say that the floor is cold and I should have some carpet on? There is no carpet on my floor, Mr. Telly, and, while on the subject, I do not even have a television set nor do I have a car. Is that luxury? It is very, very far from luxury. But I will give you a definite answer—No, I do not live in luxury. No, I do not have a big income as you seem to imagine, or, let me be fair to you, as some of your colleagues seem to imagine. To start with, some publishers in England take as much as fifty per cent from my small royalties before I get anything. Then, of course, there are agents' fees. Incidentally, the agents' fees are an investment because my agent, Mr. Stanley Knight, saves me an awful lot of work; he keeps me on the right path!

'If a book is published in a different country there may be two sets of agents' fees, and then there is tax. In addition, of course, there are all manner of expenses connected with book writing, typewriter, typing, copying, and all the rest of it.

'If the complaint is that I live in this particular apartment building, well, let me tell you this; it is cheaper living here than in many other apartment buildings. There are many advantages to living in a place such as this. I have no car, as I told you, for the simple reason that I cannot afford one, but one exceptionally good advantage in being here is that there are doormen, people who keep away unwanted, uninvited guests. People come here and unless they can produce some conclusive evidence that I am willing to see them, they are just told, "No, no admittance," and to me that is worth quite a lot of money.

'But if you really want to know what I do with the small amount of money I get I will tell you; I do research. I am doing research into the matter of the human aura. All humans have an aura around the body. There is no point in going into details here because all that is written about in considerable detail in my book *You—Forever*. If people could photograph the human aura then they could tell in advance about illnesses which were likely to affect this physical body, tell in advance while the illness was preventable or curable. You see, illness shows in the colours of the aura long before it manifests itself in the physical body. Research, equipment, costs a lot of money, and because I spend so much on research I have little indeed left for myself. Sometimes, not even enough for medical necessities.

'By the way, let me just interject my own remarks here for the moment, apart from questions. I cannot understand why all these personal and impertinent questions are asked. I write true books and it does not mean that because a reader pays a few cents for a book he has the right to enquire into my private life. Why should I not write to some of my readers and ask how much money they make and what they do with it? And why should I not ask about their sex life? Do you think they would answer that? But no matter, let us get on with these questions and answers because I have already told you I will answer some more.'

Q: 'You say you are a monk. Then why are you living with two women?'

A: 'Now that really is an utterly absurd question. Why shouldn't I live with two women? Doesn't the Pope, for instance, have women around him? He does, you know; he has a Housekeeper for one. But anyway, why not say that I live with four females? Two of the females are Siamese cat ladies and real ladies they are, too. But I have already made it clear about my sex life, or, to be more precise, my lack of sex life, so there is no point in going further into that except to point out that even Gandhi had women attendants. Christ had women about Him, and if we are to believe the Bible Christ even mixed with prostitutes. So what is wrong in mixing with women? They are humans, aren't they? You will find that in Tibet some monks were even married and their wives lived in the lama-series. No, I cannot help pondering upon the reason for such a stupid question.'

Q: 'Why did you come to Canada? The Press in England said you had gone to your Canadian hide-out. Did you come here just to hide?'

A: 'Why did I come to Canada? Why not? I have to live somewhere, and if I had gone to Timbuctoo some clot would have said, "Why did Lobsang Rampa live in Timbuctoo?" After all, why do people live in Canada? Is there anything wrong with the place? Is it a crime to live here? The answer is that I live in Canada for probably the same reason as you do; I live here because I want to live here. I have taken out Canadian citizenship and now I am a full citizen of this Canada.'

Q: 'Why are you so anti-social? Why do you live like a hermit? Why don't you meet people? Are you afraid, or something?'

A: 'You know, I would love to stop here and have a jolly good laugh. But time is pressing so let us get on with a sensible answer to a foolish question. I live as a hermit because I am utterly sick and tired of senseless questions and senseless people asking senseless questions. I have had people visit me and I have been absolutely sickened by their selfishness. They say, "Oh, what you can do for me! I want you to do this, I want you to do that." People rarely ask what they can do for me. And another thing; before I learned by hard bitter experience I did see a few people, but many of them went away from me and completely misreported everything that had happened. Some tried to make money out of the Press and they went along and sold misinformation for quite a packet of money. Now I have decided that there is no reason why I should pander to the senseless curiosity of people. I am not a freak in a cage, nor am I a sideshow attraction in a circus. So I do not and I will not see people.

'I am not afraid to meet people. Why should I be? I have

90

told all there is to be told in my books. But then again, why should I meet people if I don't want to? Do you, Mr. Telly, meet everyone who thinks they can just drop in and waste your time? Why should I meet people when so many are just trying to criticize me or trying to get something for nothing? It seems to be thought that because I write books which people can buy for a few cents, that I have to put myself up as a sort of Aunt Sally and answer any fool question, or see any mentally bereft person who can manage to totter to my door. Let me state finally that people do not have a right of access to see me, they do not have a right to come and see me whenever they think they will.

'I must tell you this, it has overtones of humour to it; when I lived in a different apartment here I had a man come to my door after midnight. He was from a Middle Eastern country and he arrived with quite a few suitcases. He came to the door and when it was opened he tried to get inside, saying, "I have come to live with you as your son." Well, that's something eh? Eventually we got rid of him, but I saw him much later in the morning, and he went away apparently satisfied.

'Some months after I received a blackmail demand for $2,000 and a very savage demand that I should embrace and write about some pecular religion that I had never even heard of before. He was very insistent that I should write books in praise of that religion. This was quite fantastic to me, but serious to him, and I have never been easily intimidated so, unfortunately for the man concerned, he quite accidentally enclosed an indication of his address on about his sixth letter to me—the first letters were quite anonymous. Anyway, I got in touch with the U.S. Postal Inspection Department and with the Police of the relevant area.

'The gentleman concerned was living in the U.S.A. illegally.

'He is not there now!

'While still on the subject I can tell you this; I have had people who have come to me in the greatest distress and have written to me claiming that the most dreadful things were going to happen to them and only I could save them. So, out of compassion, I have agreed to see them. One woman immediately wanted to jump in bed with me, an offer which I refused, and so incurred her enmity. She has ever since been trying to harm me. But others said they invented the whole thing because they knew that without very good reason I would not see them. Because of treachery of this nature I do not see people any more.'

Q: 'You have a business in England making Touch Stones and phonograph records. How do you say that you are poor when you have these business interests which bring you in money?'

A: 'No. I do not have a business in England or anywhere else in the world. I have no business interests of any sort except in writing my books and Mr. Knight, my wonderfully reliable Agent, looks after that business for me! But of course there are Touch Stones being made, and I designed them, but it is not my business and I am no part of the business.'

Q: 'The Press here—publishes a letter which they say is from the Dalai Lama and saying that you were a fake. What do you say about that?'

A: 'The Press made much of a purported statement by some secretary employed by the Dalai Lama to the effect that I was not genuine, but the Dalai Lama himself has never said such a thing, nor has his secretary said I am not genuine. The letter, for example, said he places "no credence", which is a horse of another colour. But let us look at this matter; anyone with even the meanest intelligence would know that people in "high places" have quite a number of secretaries. Leaders of countries have several secretaries, and sometimes these secretaries have limited authority to write what they consider to be fit because their employers do not have time to deal with all the correspondence themselves. So if the fellow has a personal dislike then he gets a wonderful opportunity to vent his spite on the object of his dislike and, in this particular case, I state absolutely that there is a secretary to the Dalai Lama who has no liking for me at all, and so this secretary makes remarks about "we place no credence——" which is quite a different thing from what the Press try to convey.

'By the way, you have just told me yourself that there were two "lamas" discussing the Rampa affair and one "lama" was supposed to be very opposed to me and the other was absolutely fervid in his support. Yet the Press, of course, take the side of the opposition. Why?

'There is a very well-known American author who went to see the Dalai Lama in India, and when Mr. B. came back he sent me a special message to the effect that when Tibet was free again the Dalai Lama would gladly welcome me to the Potala. No, do not place words in the mouth of the Dalai Lama which he has not uttered. Instead, regard the backstairs secretaries as suspects. You don't know their motives? Perhaps I do!

'Once again I will make another remark which doesn't, so far, come in your questions, but I gather you have a whole bunch of the wretched things. The Press seem to be very confused about my identity. But why? Look at some well-known cases—who was Shakespeare? Who was Bacon? Who was Moses? I mention these merely because they are so well known, and again, just to show how remarkable some Press statements are, I have already mentioned a Press statement about Christ going to Japan after He "ran out" on His brother. Well, what do you think about all that? Do you believe all this? It is in the Press you know. But if one is to believe all the muck the Press publish about me, well—why not believe all muck published about everyone?'

Q: 'How old are you? Why do you refuse to give your age?'

A: 'But I do refuse to give my age. It's nothing to do with anyone else. My age, which is far more than you would believe, does not affect my book writing, it doesn't add any proof to anything, and in any case I do not want to give any proof because I just couldn't care less about pleasing the Press. The ordinary decent people who read my books do believe me, but as is always the case an extremely noisy minority make a commotion quite impossible to credit unless one is the victim. But the answer is—No, I will not give my age, and the sole reason is because I do not want to!'

CHAPTER SIX

It was very tiring answering these questions. The old man lay there propped up on his bed and Mr. Telly was sitting on the foot of the bed shuffling a great sheaf of papers, and all the time he was continually fishing fresh scraps of paper out of his pocket, papers with fresh questions. Ever and anon inspiration would strike him and he would grab a pencil and write out yet another question. When he was not writing out questions Mr. Telly was doodling. He was a great doodler, and his doodles were most, most revealing!

'Well, come on then, let's get on with these questions,' said the old man, 'what's the next one?'

Q: 'If you are so strong and know so much, why can't you cure your illness?'

A: 'Now that really is the depth of absurdity. Let me tell you something; fifteen years ago I went to one of the most famous London hospitals. There I was very carefully examined, and the opinion was made that I had not more than six months of life remaining. I then went to another equally famous London hospital. They confirmed the estimate of the first, and that was more than fifteen years ago.

'Two and a half years ago in Canada I was told that I had not more than two or three months of life left. Two and a half years ago that forecast was made. Let me tell you something which may not have occurred to you; all the Press persecution is not helping my health in any way, but even the greatest of faith healing will not grow an arm or a leg which has been amputated, not even the greatest faith or medical science can grow a lung which has been removed. So whatever silly sort of person asked a fool question like that?'

Q: 'The French Press say that you probably copied Madame Blavatsky. Did you? Or if you did not copy her, then you must have copied Alexandra David-Neil. Is that correct?'

A: 'This really does seem to be a comic session, doesn't it? No, I have not copied anyone. I have no books of reference. I have never read any of the works of Madame Blavatsky nor any of the works of this Alexandra David-Neil. I write exclusively from my own personal knowledge and experience, and that seems to be entirely adequate. But why do you not read Madame Blavatsky and David-Neil and see if my books are similar. If they are, then do please come and tell me because I shall be most interested!'

Q: 'Here is a report from a French newspaper in which they say you were hired by Hitler to go to Tibet to learn all you could then you could return to counsel Hitler on how to win the war.'

A: 'Well, do you seriously think I am going to answer a question like that?! I will, though, although you do seem to have been combing the mental homes to find the most crazy people to ask the most crazy questions.

'No, I have never been hired by Hitler to go to Tibet. If you want to know the truth, the real truth, and nothing but the truth, then read all my books which are in print then you will know the truth.'

Q: 'Will you tell us some of the questions you are asked, reincarnation, for instance, people don't understand it. Transmigration, people don't understand that either. So will you answer questions about that?'

A: 'Well, I don't know what else there is to tell you. I have told you that if you read all my books you will know all this stuff, that's what my books are about. If people read my books they will know about transmigration, they will know about reincarnation, they will know about the aura.'

Q: 'Well, won't you give us just one thing about changing bodies? What is it like?'

A: 'I'll tell you what I will do; I will let you have an extract from *The Rampa Story*, you can print it and then you will get the actual incident recounted for you.'

Q: 'Why have you kept things concealed so much about a

changeover and all that? Why not come out into the open about it?'

A: 'Wait a minute. Now here is an extract from *The Third Eye* which was copyrighted in 1956. This particular extract I will pass over to you. Perhaps you will be kind enough to publish the statement in full and then it will clearly be understood that even since 1956 I have been making things "open" and I have not been "concealing things".'

Q: 'But why is your name now Rampa? What did you change it for?'

A: 'You'd be surprised! I went to South America, to Uruguay as a matter of fact, and they seemed not to believe it possible for a person to have two names, a pen name and an identity name, so they would not let me have mail which came for one name. They told me that I had to stick to one name, so I made a legal deed of name change, a change made specifically according to law. It is a perfectly legal thing and my only name now is Tuesday Lobsang Rampa. Yes, you can have a copy of the legal deed and you can publish it.

'Oh, you don't mean to say you've got another load of questions there! I thought we'd got rid of all this lot. But I do want to tell you that we'd better get these questions settled here and now because after this I am not prepared to answer any more questions, so if people do not want to believe—well, let them disbelieve. It is like taking a horse to the water; you can take a horse to the water but you cannot make him drink. You can give a person absolute irrefutable proof but you cannot make him believe if he doesn't want to believe or if he's got a closed mind. Well, what's the next question?'

Q: 'Many people ask serious questions and they don't get any answers. They ask about this business of transmigration. Well, actually, what is it? How is it done?'

A: 'But good gracious me, I have gone into this so much that I am thoroughly sick of the whole thing. It is all given in my books, you know, and it is incredible to me that you cannot get down to it and read the books. That is why they are written! But what is transmigration?

'Well, it is a cross-migrate. It just means that one soul leaves one body and takes over another body which has just at

96

that same instant been vacated by its previous occupant. There is nothing at all difficult in it. It is done very frequently. But let us start a bit further back.

'If we are to believe in a God or in a Supreme Being of any kind then we must believe in the essential goodness, the essential fairness of such a Being. Now if we are to believe that—and I am only putting it like this because you are so appallingly ignorant of the whole thing—then surely we have a right to expect that a beneficent God will be fair to all, so why should a person be born to a very high estate and have everything he wants, have no troubles, no persecution from the Press, no hatred, and another person of about the same age is born perhaps with serious illness and in poverty, and at the same time press hoodlums persecute him if he looks the wrong way or something? They both live and they both die, one to acclaim, one to sorrow. If we are to believe in a just God that cannot be, and in any case, there are definite evidences, established cases, where bodies have been switched over. You see, bodies are just vehicles. The Western science is now groping towards the truth which the Easterner has known for centuries. Man is a vehicle of a Higher Being, Man is controlled by a soul or Overself—call it what you like. Let us call it a soul because unless you have studied this a bit you could be led astray. I think you have been led astray by being a member of the Press, but that is another thing altogether. However, when a person is in the soul state he is in a much more glorious state, a state where he cannot suffer pain or suffer from vindictive persecution, but it may be necessary for him to learn something and the only way to learn, really, is by a certain amount of suffering. Suffering can be overdone, from my own experience I say that it can be overdone. But this soul selects a body to occupy when it comes down to this Earth. If you want to go touring then you select a car which will give you ample power and will carry you safely through possibly the backwoods. You will have a car which is proved to be of a reliable type, you want a good plodding work-horse of a car. Or if you want to go in for racing you will have a much more temperamental affair for race cars are temperamental indeed. But just as you would select a car for the conditions you have in mind and for the things you want to do, so the soul selects a body which will give him the range of experience he has to endure or surmount.

'Now when one is on the Other Side of life much can be seen of probabilities on this Earth. It is much the same as one can be on the ground in a little wood with trees all around you. You think you are in a vast forest, you can't see very far because you have this wood about you, and perhaps you are circumscribed by a river or perhaps you may be on a small island. If you are, then that island may be as your entire world, but if you pass over in an aeroplane you think—that mighty forest, well, it is just really a small copse. The island which was your entire world is just a spot in somebody's farm lot. That is how you would see things from the Other Side of life.

'Of course, jealous authors and idiotic pressmen are a decided nuisance when one is on this Earth, but they will have to go through it themselves in a future life. It might teach them something, and if it doesn't they will come back time after time until they do learn. But this is taking us away from transmigration, so let us get back to our cars.

'Let us say you are touring and you have reached some distant place. Circumstances urgently require that you should do something necessitating a special type of vehicle. It might be a race car, it might even be a bulldozer, but the whole point is that you, the soul of the car, get out of your touring car and you, the soul, move over to—what shall we say? A racing car or a bulldozer?—Let us say you move over to the bulldozer. You get in the thing, you do certain actions, and the bulldozer bursts into life. You, the soul, make known to the machine that which you need to have done. You steer the vehicle, you pick up all sorts of impressions from it, especially if you drop the thing into a big dip! But you are in much the same position as a soul taking over a different body.'

Q: 'Yes, but why should a man want to take over the body of another? That is a thing people ask—why does one person take over the body of another?'

A: 'I thought it was perfectly obvious. I have tried to make it clear enough. But let us take the instance to which you are so obliquely referring. Here we have a person who most desperately needed a body so that he could continue with a task which had been set for him by others, a task not at all of his choice, not at all to his liking, but a task set at the insistence of others. His own body, through the cruelty of humans, was in danger of collapse. His own body was too old, too tattered, and too unsatisfactory for the task to be carried out through its assistance.

'Now let us look at the other body; that was of a person who was heartily sick of life, a very sensitive person whose sensitivities had been beaten down by many unfortunate circumstances in his own life. He was a defeated man, a failure, if you like, but what may seem to be a failure to you was not a failure in his case. He may be the gainer in this, and you, who have tried to impede the task, well, you sure will be the loser. But anyway, this other body had a soul who was sick of living on Earth, who, some time before, had taken a wrong Path and so he knew that his own task would not be completed in that particular life. He had contemplated suicide, he hoped to die, he wished that he could will himself to death, he wasn't happy. Yet his particular body vibrated on a fundamental harmonic of that other body which was falling to pieces. It was a body which would be compatible.

'Let me digress for a moment and remind you that you may like a car very much indeed, and then you may get into another car and it will remind you strongly of the car you just left, you get on with that particular car. But if you had moved from your own car to the famous brand X, you might have found that it just did not suit your own temperament. So, while it would work just as it would for everyone else, you still would not be entirely at ease with it, not entirely happy with it, and all the time you would wish you had something better to suit you, more compatible with you, not necessarily better engineering or better condition but something better in the compatibility line. So in this instance this particular person was able to contact the occupant of a body and an arrangement was made. You will find it all in *The Rampa Story* so why we have to keep on groaning away about this particular subject I just don't understand. It has been written, it has been discussed, and throughout living history there have been many cases of transmigration.'

Q: 'Yes, that seems clear enough but it still isn't absolutely clear why this particular body was taken.'

A: 'I confess that I am not at all clear about your question! Supposing Body Y had been taken instead of Body Z, for example. You would have been asking the same thing again—why take that body? But I have already tried to make it clear to you; because the two bodies had a fundamental frequency, a fundamental vibration, because they were compatible with each other, because the "controls" were similar, because, as controls were similar, immediate take-over would be easy, because the body was there ready to be vacated, and because the person was so willing and anxious. What more can one say? The significance of this case is that the body was there at the right time for the right purpose and so it was not necessary to be like the gentleman of old who wailed and wailed, crying, "My horse, my horse, my kingdom for a horse!" The "horse" or, more properly, "vehicle" was there. And that is all there is to it. The fact that the person was married was just a side issue and—well, I suppose it wasn't adequately considered, and as it turned out things were entirely satisfactory.

'By the way, you know, you are asking a lot of questions. Now, why shouldn't I ask a question or two and get your answers? So here is something which I want to know: You and I have been quite good friends and I thought there was loyalty in friendship. I have tried to help you, but ever since we heard this affair, this report, your attitude has been very antagonistic. But I am the same person. There is nothing coming out now that didn't come out some twelve or thirteen years ago, so why have *you* changed? We have heard that some jealous person and his immature cohorts are going to write a book about me because this particular person feels resentful that my books sell. Well, I am still wondering why your attitude has changed so much, why you seem so antagonistic towards me. I am not antagonistic towards you because I can see a bit further than the mere superficial shell which surrounds most people. So, do you have any worthwhile comment which I can put in the book which I am writing for the English reading world? You see, for many years I have been attacked and attacked by a moronic type of person who knows nothing about the subject, who has never bothered to read my books. For example, some several years ago a boy committed suicide in England and just because a copy of *You—Forever* was found near him the book was labelled "the murder book". But I state definitely in all my books that I am greatly opposed to suicide. Suicide is no way out, it is the way back. And yet the Press, of which you are a member, attacked me and said that I was encouraging suicides. I got in touch with the Press in England and challenged them to show me any place in any of my books where I in any way encouraged or condoned suicide. They did not take up my challenge. Now, are you going to take up my challenge? Have you truly read all my books? All the salient facts about me are given in *The Rampa Story*. Have you read it? Then, if you have read it, why has your attitude changed so much towards me? Now it seems to me that you regard me as some particularly offensive effluvia which the dog has just dragged in. I have my feelings just as you do, perhaps even a little more. So, there it is. Now the ball is passed to you.

'But let us leave that for the moment and get on with these other things which apparently puzzle the great brains of the Press.

'You say, I believe, "Why don't I remember my out-of-body experiences?"

'I get a lot of letters and a tremendous number of people who have read my books write to me and tell me that they now do remember their out-of-body experiences. So, as one progresses, one does remember. Once you remember properly then you always remember properly. The thing is this; down on Earth the average person is not meant to remember his out-of-body experiences, nor is he intended to remember what he or she was in a past life or a past, past life, and that is rightly so because if a man had been a king in a far-distant life and he was now a beggar, then he would find his position intolerable, it might even make him too much of an arrogant beggar. So isn't it true that there is somewhere a sentence written about those, who having drunk of the Waters of Leith, forget the past that they may live in the present in preparation for the future? I have read something about it. But it is a kind

101

provision of Nature, or of God, if you like, to give people temporary forgetfulness of the past so that they may live in the future, and the present.

'You see, I started this off by saying that if we are to believe in a good God then we have to believe that there must be some sort of recompense for those who come as beggars and sufferers. Otherwise, if there is only one life, how can you, Mr. Pressman, explain the fairness of a God who lets one person come as a very wealthy man with all the position and power he wants and no troubles, and another comes as a deformed person, perhaps even mentally impaired, and in poverty? If there is only one life then quite clearly it would be an injustice to the under-privileged person, and too much favouritism for the one who had everything. Of couse that is just one aspect of the thing. There are various proofs which have been established in Indian religions about the truth of reincarnation. Christianity, you know, is quite a modern religion compared to some of the Indian religions, and actually the Indian religions are the forerunners of the Christian. It is known that Christ took over the body of Jesus—"And the Spirit of the Lord entered unto Jesus"—and then Christ "wandered in the Wilderness". Sure He did, He went to the Far East, He went through India, He went through Tibet, He met with the wise men of the time, and He formulated from all the religions He had studied a religion which at that time seemed to be most suitable for the people of that time. So that Christianity, as devised by Christ, was a mixture of Oriental religions as well as the religions of Mythology.

'But then in about the Year 60 many of the priests who rushed to jump on the band-wagon and get in on the ground floor, so to speak, thought they were losing power because of the simplicity and purity of the Christian religion, and so they messed about with the religion. They decided what they were going to have taught, and in many cases it was the complete opposite of what Christ taught. Christ was not a woman hater, He did not think that women were unclean. In fact if you study the real records you will find that Christ was a married man with a family, but that is a fact that is carefully, carefully hidden, and Christian "experts" like to keep such information from the ordinary people because they think that Christianity would then lose some of its mystique.

'But you still cannot get over this business of reincarnation? Well, I am not going to prove anything. There is proof, you know, there quite definitely is proof, but I have found in the past few years that one just cannot prove anything to a person who doesn't want to have the proof. It is like taking a horse to the water; you can take the creature to the water but you can't make him drink. If you try to he just chokes. So I say there is proof of reincarnation for those who will study Eastern and Oriental religions, but if you people can't even bother to read my books before condemning me then how are you going to study Hindu, Brahmin, Muslim, etc., religions? The best that you can do is to just give it up and wait until bitter experience teaches you that there is a bit more to all this than you had thought up to the present.

'Now, you have a question here which I thought I had already answered.'

Q: 'What am I doing wrong? Why are we not taught about the fact of living again and again?'

A: 'But surely we have already been dealing with all that almost *ad nauseam*! Wait a minute—where is that question again?—"Why are we not taught about the fact of living again and again?"'

'Well, people used to be, and I am referring to Christian people now. It used to be a part of the Christian doctrine. People puzzle over, "In my Father's house there are many mansions," but they do not understand what it really means. What it actually means is many planes of existence, many levels of astral life.

'In the old days when Christianity started and when it was formed from some of the Indian religions, reincarnation was taught, the whole mechanism of it was taught, and it is still taught in Eastern countries. But unfortunately Christians regard Christianity as the only doctrine or teaching which can possibly be considered. So if you say, "Why are we not taught——?" I can say, "But you are taught. It is just that some of your teachers try to obscure the issue." Christianity is not the biggest religion numerically, so it doesn't become the most important. If you would study other religions you would find that reincarnation is taught.

'Unfortunately the Catholic belief is that it is wrong to accept the truth of anything except a remarkably rigid doctrine which was set down by priests to safeguard their own power. They made a lot of hoopla about it being a mortal sin to think for yourself. They taught that you had to believe everything that the priests tell you, lock, stock, and barrel, even when it is obviously too ridiculous for a normal person to believe. But the Catholic priests have got their public hocussed, hypnotized into a state of terror wherein they just dare not think for themselves. Even the Pope nowadays seems to think there is quite a lot wrong with the Catholic religion, that is why he is making so many changes, isn't it? And even the Dalai Lama has admitted—to the Press, I believe—that he was not a reincarnation of Chenrezi. I believe I am correct in saying that he gave the complete circumstances of how he was picked to be this Dalai Lama. But anywhere if you study you will find out—yes, there is the truth of reincarnation available for those who are prepared to accept the truth and who do not go about with their eyes glued shut.'

Q: 'Why do we live beset by problems?'

A: 'If you go to school, if you go to college, you have problems all the time and you have to solve the problems. You go to school to learn things and to learn how to solve problems. If you are in the Arithmetic class, for instance, you are given a problem about a man who can mow a field in so many days, but how quickly will the field be mowed if you use three and a half men and a dog, or stuff like that. It is all questions. It might seem utterly stupid while you are at school, but afterwards you find that you can apply the solution of the problem to other problems which occur in the greater life beyond the school. In the same way, down on this Earth there are all manner of problems and the more evolved a person becomes the harder his problems become. But then when he goes to the Greater Life beyond this Earth, beyond all thought of returning to this Earth by way of reincarnating, then he finds that the knowledge he gained on this Earth with his problems helps him in other spheres of activity.

'If there were no problems on Earth then there would be no point in living here. If people just sat about all day and played with money or other things that money could buy, they would not be learning anything, they would be idling away their time. So instead a person gets more and more problems, and the further he progresses and evolves the greater his problems become. In the same way, in a school a University graduate would have no problem at all with the questions set the First Grader or the Kindergarten people, but the problems of the Undergraduate would be completely beyond the comprehension of the Kindergarten child. So the difficulties which a person encounters are not an indication that he is a bad person, that he is having to pay for sins committed in the past; instead it is an indication, pure and simple, that he has evolved enough so that he can be tested by quite difficult examinations.

'So when I tell you that you are adding to my problems, well—I am learning how to solve them! But all the injustice that you are showing to me will have to be paid back by you. If you want money and you don't want to work for it, then you can only borrow it from someone, but it has to be paid back with interest. And I tell you in all seriousness, all the hatred that has been directed at me by misguided people who condemn without hearing the story for the defence—well, all that is going to come back on those haters plus accrued interest. Now, that is not a fairy tale, that is a fact, as you will find out. You will find out, too, in your own hour of need that loyalty, friendship, are things beyond price. If you do not give loyalty, if you do not give your friendship, when your time of trouble comes you will find that you lack the loyalty and the friendship which would help you in your difficulties. It will come for sure. Just make a note of it when this book is published, keep it in front of you, put a book-marker in, and then you see if you don't get some troubles and you find that people whom you trusted are not loyal to you.

'You see, the whole position is this; I have done nothing wrong. I have told the truth all the way through. I have concealed nothing. And yet the Press, of which you are a member, has set itself up as accuser, judge, jury, and executioner. But I am not dead yet, I have a lot more active life in me. I can only say to you of the Press that it might be very profitable for you to read your Christian Bible, read Exodus, Chapter 22—21 which reads, "Thou shalt neither vex a stranger, nor oppress him: For ye were strangers in the Land of Egypt." But in place of "Egypt" why not put "Canada"? I am sure it would be applicable.

'Here is a further question which apparently originated with the Press:

Q: 'Do animals go to the spirit world and do we see them again? Do they have souls and intelligence?'

A: 'Animals have intelligence? Good gracious me, yes! Some of them are more intelligent than some humans. My little Siamese cat, Cleopatra, is truly the most intelligent little person I have met. She shows high intelligence and high appreciation. And Tadalinka is exceptionally clairvoyant and telepathic, and you can't say that for most humans, can you?

'Yes, animals go to the spirit world. If we are to assume the existence of a God—and how can *we* exist without a God?— then we must agree that little animals and big animals too have their rights, have their right to be considered by a God, because humans are only one specialized form of animal, a more savage form than is common among animals. It is said that only humans and spiders commit rape. That's worth a thought, too. But animals—yes, they go to the astral world in precisely the same manner as do humans. They are born again and again, but of course each species reincarnates according to its own classification. That is, humans do not become animals and animals do not become humans. They are different things altogether. But again, if you have read all my books you will have read about cats and what they do in this life.

'It is only Christians who deny that animals have souls. But then most Christians show little appreciation for their own souls. They do whatever they can to harm others, always ready to take the advantage, but animals do not do that. Animals kill only to eat, they do not murder for money and all that sort of thing. They live according to the Law of Nature which is how they have to live, but you have never heard of an animal going out shooting partridges or duck just for the fun of it. You have never seen animals rushing along a road trying to run down a weaker animal just for something to do. But humans do that. The answer to your question is—yes, animals have souls, animals have intelligence. And, yes, if a human and an animal want to meet on the Other Side of life then they can do so provided both want it because the human is not the Lord of Creation. In other worlds and in other existences humans are not much more than the earthworms are on this world.'

Q: 'Why will you not see people? Why will you not be more sociable and mix with people?'

A: 'Well, I have already answered this. I have already told you that everyone has a right to decide if they are going to meet people or not meet people and quite bluntly, why should I meet Press people? My attitude about the Press is this; Press people go out of their way to try to prove me false, to try to prove that I write lies. But my dear man, fancy the Press—the *Press*—of all people, doing this! Who are they to set themselves up as judges? Before the Press can write about the lies or alleged lies of others they should make sure that their own conscience is clear. It has come to a bad thing, you know, when the Pope and Bishops and other equally important people have to ask the Press to be more truthful. And yet, these are the people who try to judge me. It makes me laugh!

'But you know, there is a very good reason for remaining what I can only term "solitary". I have different abilities, different powers, because, at risk of repeating myself, I am going to tell you that all my books are true and I can do every one of those things that I write about, but that means I have different sensitivities from the average. I cannot do some of the things which the average person takes for granted, but because I live alone I develop other senses. Look at it like this; if a person is blind then he develops an increased sense of touch or an increased sense of hearing which, in some degree, compensates for the loss of sight. Again, if people live in a herd then they all come down to the common herd level, but if a man goes away into the wilderness for a time he finds that his senses became far more acute, his sight becomes more acute, his hearing becomes more acute, and so does his sense of smell. Trackers who live in the wilds have a very, very keen set of senses, in fact some of the aborigines in Australia can track a man several days after he passed that way when there is no sign of anything at all unusual to the average white man.

'So if a person is going to develop and retain special abilities he has to live alone. If he mixes too much then his sensitivities become blunted. You find monks living as recluses will get increased power. They become telepathic or clairvoyant, but they call it communing with God or similar. Actually it is just that which happens in the normal course of events.

'But if you wish to develop then you have to be alone and that is about all there is to it. Perhaps I should say that what really happens is that when you get a lot of people together you get some with negative auras, others with positive auras, some with strong thoughts and some with bad thoughts, everything is mixed up and it leads to a depletion of nervous energy. How many times have you felt drained, depleted, tired out after going and mixing with a lot of people? Suppose you go to a big party—everyone is drinking and chattering and dancing about from place to place. It may be all right while you are there, but afterwards you feel drained, you get a hangover or something and you think it is solely the fault of the alcohol, but it is not; it is through draining of the nervous energy through mixing with so many people of conflicting auras.

'Suppose you got a whole bunch of magnets and you tossed them in a pile together. Some would cling to some, and others would be repelled, depending, of course, on which way their poles were facing, that is, whether they were positive or negative. And people are just the same as that because the vehicle called a human is, after all, just an electric device. There are brain waves—well, it is admitted nowadays that there are brain waves, it is admitted that thoughts can be charted with squiggly lines on paper and brain voltages can be readily measured. So all these are in conflict when they are too mixed up with the others.

'Every person has a basic note—I might call it a music note except that some of the frequencies are not too musical after all—but every person emits a noise, a noise like static with a hum behind it. You may have heard something like this if you got close to a bee hive. But people buzz, and tick and hum, and humans are so utterly used to it that they no longer notice

108

it. In the same way, every race has its own distinctive smell. White people cannot get too close to black people, they say, because they allege that the black people smell, but usually the black people are far too polite to turn around to the white person and say, "Well you stink a jolly sight worse!" But it is true. Everyone has their own race-smell upon which is super-imposed that person's own particular aroma, and every person also emits a note which can be detected by instruments and the note is the note of that person's race on which is superimposed the person's identity-note. The two may result in harmony or discord, and if it is discord then the person is very hard to associate with because one has the feeling of being badly drained, one has the feeling that always in association with that person there is an unfortunate clash of personalities.'

Q: 'What do you really think about meditation?'

A: 'Meditation is a very real, very necessary thing. Ameri-can researchers have recently found that when a person is in a state of meditation his general metabolic responses are consid-erably affected, his blood changes, his general being changes, and all this can be detected very readily by instruments. The worst thing about meditation is all the rubbish being written about it. All these cults, correspondence courses, etc., etc., are absolutely unnecessary, you don't need all this guff to help you to meditate. It seems that the only help is to help the bank account of the one who is teaching meditation. Meditation is natural, it is as natural as breathing, it is as natural as think-ing. But the fantastic tales which go around about how to meditate and what meditation is—well, it is enough to put anyone off. One of the biggest difficulties, of course, is that there are so many fakes in occult work, but that again is the fault of people because if people as a whole would be more open-minded then definite research could be done in the mat-ter of investigating what was genuine and what was not genu-ine. This is a thing about which I feel very strongly. We send men into space, which is quite unnecessary, because it could all be done by astral travel with far, far better results. But any-way, men are sent into space but no money at all is being spent on investigation of what comes after death. Is there really astral travel? I know there is, of course, but it could be investigated for the ordinary man or woman in the street. If scientists would keep an open mind then those with genuine abilities would gladly co-operate to demonstrate their abilities.

'Now we get a case where a self-styled "researcher" brow-beats a genuine psychic person and says, "Okay you perform for me and I'll do my best to prove you are a fake. I don't believe what you do and I will prove that it is all a fake." In such conditions proof cannot be given because some of the occult sciences are very delicate things indeed, very fragile things indeed, they have to have the right conditions. You wouldn't suddenly say to a photographer, "Okay, I'm coming into the darkroom with you to see exactly what you are doing," and then go into the darkroom and switch on all the lights. That would ruin whatever the photographer was trying to do, and it would be too stupid for words. So, if there is to be proof there would have to be researchers who were sympathetic. They would not have to commit themselves to believing, mind, but they would have to be sympathetic, they would have to keep an open mind and be ready to accept. It is the brutality of the present "investigation" that shocks the psychics into re-fusing to co-operate, and of course the Press must bear the greatest responsibility for that because they come along with their blaring trumpeting voices and their hard-boiled sceptical attitudes and they are not ready to believe anything even if it is proved. If a thing is proved beyond any genuine doubt, then the Press will insist that there must be trickery somewhere and it's just too bad that for the moment they can't point out where or what it is.

'Anyway, the time will come when it will be necessary to carry out a proper investigation into what is death, what comes after death. The Press say you can't weigh a soul; no, but who wants to, a soul is in a different dimension, they are using the wrong yardstick. Everyone consists of a bunch of vibrations just as a radio signal is, in effect, a vibration or a frequency or a wavelength. Humans are on part of a certain spectrum. While down here on Earth we have weight, we can feel resistance if we poke something which we consider to be solid. But if we go into a different dimension then the things that down here are solid are no longer solid, in fact they may be so insubstantial

110

that they cannot be perceived at all. A similar thing happens to the other side of the scale; a soul departs from a body but it is on a different time, a different dimension, and so the crude three-dimensional equipment cannot detect it.

'When we get scientists who will listen to the advice of occultists as to how things can be tested, then indeed adequate proof will be coming forward because there are genuine occultists. There are, of course, many fakes, but there are quite definitely thousands of genuinely occult people who can do what they claim to do. They should be preserved and the fakes should be weeded out.'

Q: 'How do you say one should learn to meditate?'

A: 'I have gone into that quite a lot in my books. There is no difficulty at all in it. The main difficulty is caused by people who won't believe how easy it is. They want to work hard at it and so they are so busy working hard at it that they don't get results. If you want to know how to meditate then read my books. After all, even the Press should read the books before they attempt to express any opinion because if they just blare out an accusation without having read the books then how can they possibly know what they are talking about? Not that they do in any case, but let us be fairly polite even to the Pressmen.'

Q: 'What is this astral travel stuff you are always talking about? Is there anything to it?'

A: 'Yes, there most definitely is, there absolutely definitely is. But it is a very difficult thing to explain to a person who doesn't want to believe, wherein the case of a sighted person trying to explain to one who was born blind the difference between, let us say, orange and pink, or two shades of green. How would you explain to a person who had never had sight what was the difference between a cabbage green and a lettuce green? Or the difference in colour between an orange and a lemon? How would you set about it?

'I have already said that you can liken the human body to a motor vehicle, and the soul or astral body, whichever you like to call it, can be likened unto the driver of the vehicle. Now, if you go out driving and then you return you switch off the engine of your car and the car stays in a certain spot. You get out and go somewhere else. That is just how it is in astral travel.

'The physical body is tired out, perhaps; you might have done a little work trying to chase up a scandal story or something and then you have had a lot of entertainment. After that you are tired and so you come home and you go to bed. That is like parking your car, you have parked your vehicle when you go to bed. Then you switch off, in other words, you go to sleep. But the driver, your soul, or your astral form, whichever you want to call it, leaves the body and goes elsewhere, it goes to a plane of existence where there are others also doing astral travel. Of course you come back to your body because you have a link, what is called the Silver Cord, which can be likened to a carrier wave in a radio programme on which the ordinary programme is superimposed.

'You get out of your physical body, then, and you travel away somewhere into the astral world. There you may meet a person whom you are going to meet in the flesh the next day, and you discuss things with that person. Then when you are back in the flesh and in the presence of the person you think, "Funny thing! I'm sure I have lived through all this before!" If you have done that, if you have made your contact in the astral, then your meeting goes very much more smoothly as if it were fore-ordained, which it probably was. Many of the world's most successful men know the secret, consciously or unconsciously, of astral travel, and they are able to make contacts in the astral so they pre-plan and prepare that which is going to be accomplished on the Earth plane in the Earth body in the following days. Because they prepared everything so thoroughly there is no problem, everything runs smoothly, all decisions are cut and dried, and everyone "falls into place" with clockwork precision.

'Oh yes, definitely there is such a thing as astral travel. It is a very simple matter, anyone can do it if they have faith and the patience to try a few elementary steps. But of course if you are going to start off with a whole load of disbelief and dislike and all that sort of thing, then you will not remember your astral travels. I state quite definitely that everyone does astral travel because you wouldn't imagine a fellow parking his car and just sitting in the thing until next day, would you? He would have to get out and stretch his legs. He would have to get out and have food or something. In just the same way every person gets out of the body and into the astral but many people do not remember their experiences because they are afraid to or because they don't believe in such things.

'Some people have dreams. Now frequently the dreams are rationalizations of what actually happened. The person is a doubter to start with and just would not believe the possibility of astral travel, and so as a solution to what would be a difficult problem the sub-conscious of the doubter cooks up a fantastic image or dream which truly is stranger than anything that could happen in real life. Dreams, then, are either the rationalization of an astral experience or the mindless wandering thoughts of a body of which the soul or astral form is away, away so far that no check is being kept in the mental processes of the sleeping form.

'Again I say, yes, you can do astral travel consciously. Everyone can do it when they sleep. Not everyone remembers it. People with a little training can do it while they are awake. It is very very interesting. The biggest difficulty is that you cannot carry anything with you, which is a bit inconvenient at times.

'So you want to ask more questions, do you? Well, in this instance I will answer your questions because as I said, I propose to use this material in the book which I am now writing for the English version and which I started about a month ago. Your first question then:

Q: 'What is your comment on pollution, its causes, its problems, its effect, and its solution?'

A: 'Undoubtedly there is a very grave problem with pollution, but of course everything is entirely manmade. Nature doesn't cause pollution, Nature tried to overcome pollution. First of all Man is depleting the atmosphere of oxygen. In Brazil one of the rain forests is being cut down and it is estimated that if that is done, as now planned, there will be in thirty years time one third less oxygen in the air than there is today. That is a very serious thing indeed because the less the oxygen, the more the pollution. So humans are committing

113

suicide in bulk.

'There are other problems which arise when forests are cut down. The Americans found that after they cut down their wooded areas they had dust bowls as the result. Trees, in addition to providing oxygen for the atmosphere, also hold the top soil together. The roots of a tree go deep into the top soil and hold the soil together so that it cannot blow away. The trees also help in the conservation of moisture in the soil. They keep the ground alive. But when the trees are cut down there is nothing to hold the soil together, the nature of the whole area changes and it becomes more arid. And so the soil dries out and because of the lack of moisture the grains of earth do not adhere together. The winds come and there is nothing to stop the winds, and they sweep across the face of the barren earth carrying off the soil. It may be blown into the rivers, it may be blown into the sea, but anyway in just a short time what was a fertile healthy region becomes a barren desert made so by Man. One of the biggest troubles with the earth is this awful petroleum muck; that is indeed a curse. Steam engines are the things because steam does not pollute and the moisture in steam returns to the earth and helps it, whereas the horrid fumes of petroleum products poison everything, everything. Look at a jet plane taking off or landing, look at the filthy stuff spewing out astern dropping an oily film over everything in its path.

'Fifty years ago there were steam propelled motor vehicles, the old Stanley Steamer for example; well, nothing can approach that at the present time. The Stanley Steamer was extremely comfortable and exceptionally fast, it had great power and it did not at any time under any condition pollute the atmosphere nor pollute the earth. But vested interests—money-mad men—killed the steam car and instead started a bit of race suicide by producing petroleum-run engines, leading to cancer and all the other types of illness to which mankind is now so very prone.

'If mankind, with its insensate lust for money, goes on producing all these devilish chemicals and synthetics, then soon there will be no life on this earth. Many of the synthetic compounds are lethal indeed. Our lakes and rivers are polluted.

114

They are just masses of flowing poison. In many areas people can no longer bathe in the rivers nor swim from the beaches because the pollution is so bad. Ships making landfall encounter great masses of floating garbage, seamen can tell right away when they are approaching land, they don't need radio because they can tell by the discolouration of the waters miles from the land.

'You ask what can be the solution. Well, there is a solution, you know, there is a solution to all our problems. Mankind will have to return to a religion. It doesn't matter what religion it is as long as it is a religion because religion gives one the necessary spiritual discipline with which one can regulate one's own acts. Truly religious people would not put money before the health of others. They would attempt to conserve life instead of just to accumulate cash. There would have to be a return to Nature, to natural things. People would have to return to the countryside instead of going off like sheep to the cities. There are vast tracts of land virtually uninhabited because people do not want to work the land, they want to stick in some stinking factory making products which poison the population. That would have to be changed. The farmers have little status in the social scheme of things, and they would have to be given status before they could again attract workers to their farms.

'Many many years ago when the Earth was young the atmosphere was very different from what it is now. Human life as we know it at present could not live under such conditions because there were sulphur vapours from raging volcanoes, there were gaseous stenches from quaking bogs where methane and all the rest of it was ejected into the atmosphere. The atmosphere, too, was much heavier, much denser than it is at present. With the passage of many, many centuries the atmosphere changed and became purer. As vegetation flourished on the Earth more and more oxygen was poured into the skies, and human life developed in a manner which could make the best use of that oxygen. But now oxygen is being denied us, pollution is being substituted, lung complaints are on the increase, health is deteriorating, and unless there be a return to the simpler things of life with an outlawing of petroleum products and an outlawing of some of these devilish synthetics,

115

human life could soon become extinct. It could become extinct by the year 2000. But every country is vying with every country to put more pollution into the skies. They call it social progress. Countries are in competition with each other; how much of the forests can be cut down to be made into paper for useless newspapers. I have long stated that the Press is the most evil force on this Earth, and I firmly believe so, and one of the ways in which the Press is evil is that it uses such a vast amount of paper. Paper—for newspaper use—comes from trees, the flesh of trees, and the greater the demand for newspapers and their sensational contents, the greater the demand for trees. And so more and more do men go out into the wilderness to search for forests which so far have not been touched.

'As the tree men go out over the land they leave a scene of desolation behind them, a scene like something on the Moon, craters where tree stumps have been pulled out, rocks where the soil is blown away. So unless the trend can be reversed, unless trees are planted instead of felled—well, you might as well say goodbye to human life, you might as well say goodbye to all life on this Earth until a new type of person can be produced which can live under these stinking conditions. It does not refer just to human life but to all life; in the seas and in the rivers fish are dying from pollution, in the air birds are dying from eating polluted fish. It all comes back—one must have a return to religion and a return to the land. Nowadays men and women rush off to work, scrabble for money. Their children, the future race, are just more or less abandoned on the streets to fend for themselves, to live under the domination of the stronger characters who, all too often, are evil characters.

'And so all the time conditions are becoming worse and worse and worse. If we want to have a beautiful orchard then one goes in for selective pruning, selective grafting, selective planting. If one wants the best type of stock—horses or cows or anything else—then one sees that the breeding is controlled. Unsatisfactory stock is not permitted to breed, to reproduce its own species of defective creature, yet humans, the "Lords of Creation", live according to a reversed order; the scruffier the human, the crummier their morals and their brain power, the

116

more children they have and the more abandoned those children are because both parents are busily scrabbling for money. But the vested interests make this artificial state of affairs. If there is going to be mass production, then there must be plenty of money to buy things. If the man only is working he either does not get enough money to buy all they want, or rather, all they think they want, or the factories do not have enough cheap labour and so women are more or less drilled into thinking that they haven't enough to live on. So mother and father, husband and wife, work in the factories and the children are neglected and the race becomes worse and worse. It is like livestock deteriorating under haphazard breeding.

'The only solution is that the leaders of the world should form some world government. The religious teachers of the world should cease fighting among themselves and they should try to do something for humanity. They should teach that salvation doesn't live in the factory but on the land, and unless there can be a return to religion then there is no hope whatever for the Earth.'

Q: 'What do you think about students' protests, all kinds of protests in Universities, etc.'

A: 'I really think that these University students have a quite inflated idea of themselves. Let us look at the question properly; if people are going to school—and a University is only a school—then it means that they don't know everything or they wouldn't be going to school. It is a matter of complete amazement to me that these students—school kids—dare to think that they have the power to set the world right. It seems to me that they should occupy their time in studying so that when they have completed their studies and passed examinations to prove it then, and then only, should they set about reorganizing the world. By that time they will know something about it so they will just put up and shut up!

'I have no sympathy whatever with these school kids who think they know so much that they can, let us say, "out-manoeuvre Churchill" and people of similar status.'

Q: 'What of strikes and unions in general?'

A: 'I think there should be no strikes. Strikes are a vicious form of blackmail. At the time I am writing this I am here in

117

Montreal which is a sick city indeed, a sick city in a sick Province where strikes and violence seem to be the everyday method of life.

'So far as I can see strikes cause the workers to lose money and the employer to lose money There should be arbitration, there should be definite legal Courts, industrial Courts which settle the problem. But in my life I have met a few Union organizers and I would prefer to call them stinking goons. It seems to me that the average Union man is scared stiff of the Union goon, enforcer, and if I were approached by any of these goons I would soon report it to the Police. But it does seem to me that the Unions are run for the benefit of the Union leaders because, from what I have heard, the more the Union leaders get for their members the more they demand for themselves. We get cases of jury tampering, we get cases where innocent work people are attacked with iron bars. Well, how can one justify the existence of Unions? I think they should be banned by Law just as strikes should be banned by Law.

'Many, many years ago in England workers had a much better system, they had Guilds who helped them and I think all workers should have specialized Guilds and not Unions. In other words, I am definitely opposed to Unions.

'Just a short time ago there was a hospital strike and more than one medical friend told me, "Oh yes, we know that many people died through that withdrawal of hospital service. But what can we do about it? We know about it, but if we try to make a case about it the Unions will call the people out on strike again and it will just be worse." I needed to go to hospital during the strike and, of course, because of the strike I couldn't go, so perhaps I am biased against such strikers. But I cannot help hoping that sometime when there is a strike some of the strikers' relatives are the losers.'

Q: 'The violence in the world—what do you think about that? What can be done about it?'

A: 'Of course the violence in the world is a simple matter to explain. People are being given false values. Religion is being torn down. People no longer believe in the simple things of life. They listen to the radio, they watch terrible things on television, and they read the gory details in the sensational Press. So people are conditioned by the radio, conditioned by television programmes, and, of course, "hotted up" by the Press who glorify in gore. You get people watching a TV programme and they see some highly mythical house in Hollywood and they think, "Why should they have a house like that and not me? I should have the same. I want a Cadillac, a houseboat, a speedboat, and an aeroplane." And so they get discontented. Discontent breeds discontent, and eventually gangs set up, robberies are done, people are kidnapped, people go in for law cases for all manner of imaginary complaints. At present one "sports woman" is suing a club for a few million dollars a few million dollars! More than she could make in ten lifetimes. But people have an altogether inflated idea of their worth. A million dollars nowadays seems hardly anything when it comes to making claims. But that, of course, is caused by the Press. The Press egg people on to do these foolish things because if the people didn't have such crazy ideas the Press would have less to write about. Many years ago I was told that the Press didn't want the truth, they wanted to print what people thought they should read. They wanted sensation, and I was told that no matter if I wouldn't give an interview, an interview would be "dreamed up".

'Here is a little example: Last week a Tibetan woman was widely quoted in the local press. It was stated that she gave an interview to the Press and said all manner of remarkable things. But the woman complained that she hadn't even met a pressman! No pressman at all had approached her. There had been no interview except in the Press reporter's imagination. Having suffered from that myself I quite believe her, and I do not believe the Press on principle.

'But the violence is caused by lack of parental supervision. The fathers and the mothers work in the factories, and after that they have to rush to the pubs or to Bingo or to anywhere else, and the children—legitimate or illegitimate—are left to fend for themselves on the streets and to be contaminated by the stronger and usually more evilly disposed youths who rise out of the maelstrom.

'Again, only a return to religion can save this world. The

119

human animal is deteriorating, becoming less and less able to decide which is right and which is wrong. The religions of the present day are staffed by men with clay feet, not able to teach religion but instead more intent on dabbling in politics and presumably getting a bit more money from that. Priests should be priests. Priests should attend to a person's soul. They should not bother with a person's politics.

'So it is. You have asked me a question, and I say that unless there be a return to religion and a definite censorship of the Press there is no real hope for humanity which is all the time deteriorating.'

Q: 'What do you think of the Viet Nam war?'

A: 'Well, I would like to heartily congratulate the Vietnamese! I think it is highly amusing that what the Americans have regarded as "poor ignorant little coloured men" can stand off first all the might of France, and now all the might of America. America cannot win in Viet Nam so long as the people there are of good spirits. What is the point of dropping a hundred thousand tons of bombs on marshland? It makes a frightfully muddy splash, agreed, but it doesn't do much harm. The real type of war is that which the Vietnamese fight—guerrilla war. And if the Vietnamese were as vicious as the Americans pretend, believe me, the Vietnamese would chase the Americans out of Viet Nam as if their pants were on fire because the Americans—well there seems to be a lot of graft out there. The Vietnamese go about their particular tasks trying to ensure that their country continues in the way they want it, not in the way the Americans want it.'

CHAPTER SEVEN

Mr. Telly gave a slight start as the old man said, 'Well, that's it. I've answered all the questions I'm going to answer.'

Mr. Telly fidgeted about, shuffled his feet, and fiddled with his doodles, then said, 'My! Why don't you have carpets on the floors? It's so cold in here. You could buy carpets cheaply, you know. Wait a minute, I'll tell you a place where you can get them at a very, very cheap price.'

The old man snorted and said, 'But I've just been explaining, I don't go in for luxuries so I am not interested in getting carpet.'

Mr. Telly fidgeted around and then he said, 'What we must do, we must get a television crew here and make a little film of you. Everybody wants to see you on TV.'

The old man nearly jumped off his bed in annoyance. 'Oh no, I'm not interested in TV. I am not interested at all in the idiot box or the idiots who watch it. I think, second only to the Press, television is the greatest curse of our time. It pretends to show people the better things of life, but instead it just gives people dissatisfaction.'

Mr. Telly said, 'Well, can I bring my Bolex cine camera here and lights, and my recorder, and you say just a few words —just a few words? It'll help me so much if you'll do just that, and it won't inconvenience you at all.'

The old man thought about it and was getting heartily sick of the whole affair. It was another of those instances of give a man an inch and he'll take a mile, but at last he said, 'All right, provided that you and you alone come, you can bring your camera and you can bring your recorder, but understand this—if you bring a television crew with you the door will not

121

be opened.'

The next day the big powerful car of Mr. Telly swooshed by with a rush of displaced air and a loud zooming noise. Minutes after he came running along the stone corridor red in the face with exertion, draped about with cameras, lights, and carrying a recorder in his hand. 'I've come—I've come,' he said, stressing what was already distressingly obvious.

With considerable expertise he set up his lights, set up his camera, and got his recorder working. He seemed to be like the mythical McNamara's Band, or a one-armed juggler. The lights were bright and Miss Cleopatra came along and sat beside the old man so that she, too, should have her photograph taken. And after Miss Cleopatra had made her debut on the film, Fat Cat Taddy was womanhandled in because Fat Cat Taddy doesn't like cameras or any interruption to her standard routine which is normally eat—rest, eat—rest, but Fat Cat Taddy had to come and be on a film as well.

The old man said his very few words in English, and Mr. Telly eventually rushed away again—he seemed to be jet-propelled always—and peace descended upon the somewhat shaken household.

Later the film was shown on French language television. Again an extremely small minority made extremely bad statements. The mail came swamping in, swamping Mr. Telly and swamping the old man, and about ninety-nine and nine-tenths per cent were in favour, were interested, etc. But just one or two petty-minded people wanted to make difficulties because the old man spoke in English and not in French, and, they said, if he did not want to speak in French then he should not have been on French language television.

It is such a pity that these French-Canadians are so insistent about their own language. After all, they want business, they are trying to do business with the U.S.A. and other countries but they are setting as a condition that U.S.A. firms and firms in other countries shall speak only in French. My own opinion, for what it is worth, is that the French language should be scrapped for business in Canada and just kept for the amusement of those few people who want to speak some form of French. It is my opinion that if a person is a Canadian, he should be a Canadian first, second, and third, he should deal with the natural language of the country, which is English, and not play games with pseudo-linguistics. I put on record here and now, I have no sympathy with French-Canadians, no sympathy with their very, very aggressive attitudes and their insistence in putting themselves forward, right in the forefront at all times irrespective of the rights and feelings of other people.

Conditions were becoming increasingly difficult. It seemed to the old man that every time he went out there was some pressman or other hiding behind every pillar. The number of callers to the door increased, all manner of strange excuses were made by which the caller hoped to get to meet Lobsang Rampa.

For several nights two men were perched like broody hens on a little wall outside the old man's bedroom window. One night they used a long, thin stick and kept tapping on the glass of the window, tapping to attract his attention so that, hopefully, he would be lured to push aside the curtains and peer out. One of the men always had his camera and flash gun ready.

That system not working they tried the other one in which one man let off flash bulbs at the window while the second man with the camera stood ready with his flash gun and camera so that a photograph could be taken. But, again, without success.

But these pressmen had all manner of nice little tricks designed—quite unsuccessfully as it happened—to lure the old man to the window so that a photograph could be taken of him perhaps in his pyjamas. Sometimes a handful of gravel would be tossed against the window. First there would come the pattering of two or three grains of sand, then two or three more, and then perhaps a handful of loose sand thrown violently and with extreme exasperation. But—no, the curtain was never drawn aside for their delectation because these people never seem to understand that there are other ways of watching people than peering out through a window. These people were so avid in their watch on just one window that they forgot there were other windows, they forgot that there were other people in other apartments who could report what was happen-

123

ing! But matters were becoming intolerable. It was extremely embarrassing to go out anywhere—to go into the city—because of the people accosting, because of people who were nodding and smiling. It was extremely embarrassing to go out in a taxi because all one's private affairs seemed now to be public affairs through the French-language newspapers and the French-language television. There was no difficulty with the English newspapers, no difficulty with the English television, only the French.

People pointing and nodding and smiling, not all ill-natured by any means. In fact, a very very small percentage were unfriendly, perhaps less than a tenth of one per cent were unfriendly, but they certainly were noisy. And everyone has a right to privacy, everyone has a right to remain aloof from others if he or she so desires to remain aloof from others, yet in Montreal there was no privacy. It seemed to be just like a village. A man at one end of the city sneezed and the report of it reached the other end by Dorval almost before the man had finished sneezing.

So a decision was reached at last. The Family would go away from Montreal, away from the Province of Quebec which had proved to be so inhospitable on the French side of it, and had proved to be so productive of troubles. The French-Canadian seemed to make a hobby of his hate, and it does seem that French-Canadians even hate French-Canadians, in fact often it appeared that they hated French-Canadians more than they hated anything else!

So this little Family, two women, and two Siamese cats, and one old disabled man sick at heart and sick in health, sat together and discussed what they should do, where they should go, and not only where they should go but how to get there because it's not easy to travel long distances with Siamese cats, furniture, and one person confined to a wheelchair.

The discussion was long. It lasted sporadically over several days. Maps were consulted, people in distant places were asked. So eventually it was decided to go to British Columbia which was about as far away as one could get from the Province of Quebec, about as far away as one could get from French-Canadians, those unlovely people. Of course there are

124

some good French-Canadians, some who are brilliant, talented, gifted. Mayor Drapeau of Montreal, a brilliant man, a humane man, and a humorous man too. Mayor Drapeau, perhaps Canada's finest French-Canadian. Then, of course, Prime Minister Trudeau, he is a French-Canadian too. But there seem to be French-Canadians *and* French-Canadians, some are not so good, and others are cultured gentlemen.

Letters were sent to Victoria in British Columbia, and letters were sent to Vancouver, British Columbia. Batches of letters were sent to Rental Agents and batches of letters were sent to Real Estate people, and not one single reply was received!

The Family pondered and pondered on the strangeness of it all. All these addresses of Rental Agents and Real Estate people, all obtained from the current Yellow Pages in the telephone directory, all contained stamped addressed envelopes for a reply, and yet—no replies. We had to wait until we got to British Columbia to find the reason for that!

Another plan was formulated. The Family would go to Vancouver and would stay in some hotel or boarding house for the time being, and they would look about and find accommodation. So contact was made with a few hotels in Vancouver and, at last, there seemed to be one who offered reasonable terms and reasonable accommodation. At about the same time a newspaper cutting was enclosed from a Vancouver newspaper, no letter with it, just a newspaper cutting. The Vancouver newspaper published a small item about the author Lobsang Rampa, author of *The Third Eye*, etc., who was coming to live at Kitsilano, Vancouver. Kitsilano where the hippies live. So the Family mulled over it and decided that they would not go to Kitsilano anyway if the Press said that that was where they were living, and at that time they hadn't the faintest idea where Kitsilano was!

Slowly arrangements were made to move. The lease of the apartment was given up and the little Family moved into a Guest Apartment while their furniture was being packed and taken away, taken away to travel by road three thousand miles across Ontario, past Winnipeg, all through the Prairies and up over the Rockies and down the other side to Vancouver where, it was hoped, yet another start could be made.

The book, *Candlelight*—this book—had been started. Now it was put away, nothing more could be done while living in a Guest Apartment, nothing more could be done while preparations were being made to travel and while the future was so black and so uncertain.

The old man trundled around in his wheelchair saying a final goodbye to one person and another and another, tenants of other apartments, tenants who had been decent, who had minded their own business, tenants who had shown that there were good people, after all, even in Montreal. One or two French-Canadians also were greeted and invited to come to Vancouver at any time and they would be welcome guests.

For a last time the old man went along in his wheelchair throughout the grounds, up by the Labyrinth and over the Bridge towards Man and His World, but even on this last trip people were difficult, a speeding car slammed to a shrieking stop as the carload of people recognized the old man. Cameras were grabbed and the old man's progress was seriously impeded while the people in the car tried to get close-ups. But an electrically propelled wheelchair is much easier to manoeuvre than a car, and the people were denied their close-ups after all. So once again the old man turned back and entered the apartment building grounds, ran his chair up the ramp to the Plaza, and along the few feet to the Guest Apartment.

'I'm not going out again in this dump,' he said to the concerned ones within the apartment. 'There's no peace at all from the crowds who throng around.' He turned away and thought back a few months to when the snow was heavy on the ground and traversing the swept ways was difficult. The old man had been out on this very rare occasion alone, and trying to get up the rubber-covered ramp to the Plaza. But the ramp was slippery and the wheelchair kept slipping backwards into a snow bank at its lower end.

Upon the Plaza itself were four French-Canadian young men laughing, jeering, deriving immense satisfaction from the sight of a disabled old man trying to live his own life, trying to get about a bit, and their mirth was intense when he couldn't get the wheelchair up the ramp because of the slippery surface. Eventually they tired of watching and just rushed away down

126

the side steps, jumped into a car and roared off sending clouds of snow from their spinning back wheels. They were of a well-known French-Canadian family.

There came the time when there was no longer any reason to stay in the Guest Apartment nor in Montreal, so in an early morning a Murray-Hill taxi came along and the two women, the two Siamese cats, and the old man got in. Their cases and the wheelchair were put in a second taxi, and off they drove to the airport of Montreal. After delays, red tape matters and so on, they eventually got aboard an aeroplane and flew all the way to Vancouver, stopping first at Winnipeg which seemed like a lost city standing sentinel in the midst of nothingness, and then over the Rockies, the Rockies which seemed like heat bumps after the mountains of the Himalayas. Soon after crossing the Rockies the plane lowered, soon there came the lumbering 'clunk' of the undercarriage being extended, then Sea Island, the Airport of Vancouver, came in sight. The plane banked, lowered, the engine notes changed and soon there was the scrunch and screech of tyres on the runway. The trundling motion of a plane on the tarmac, and eventually the tail swung around so the plane was sideways on to the terminal buildings.

Stiffly the Family got to their feet, stiffly they got out of the plane and into yet another taxi which drove them to a nearby hotel.

In passing, it is quite an experience to be a disabled person in a wheelchair. Sometimes a good airline will have a forklift truck to lift the wheelchair up to the passenger compartment. Sometimes an airline will say they have no facilities, and the disabled person has to manage the best way he can down a flight of stairs, not always easy for a person who is partly paralysed. But one of my happiest memories was in Saint John, New Brunswick, after a journey by train when I had to go from the station in Saint John to the Admiral Beatty Hotel, and there was no other way of transporting me except—on a fish truck! The attendant, or driver's assistant, was an exceptionally courteous and considerate man, I might have been his rich uncle by the care he took of me. I drove my wheelchair on to the lifting section on the tail of the truck, and this assistant was meticulous in seeing that I was on safely, that my

127

wheelchair was stopped with the brakes on and everything else. And while the tail section was going up on its hydraulic lift he hung on to the wheelchair, and I should say that that was the safest 'elevation' I have ever had. That man—I am sorry to say I do not know his name—was a real gentleman.

It was quite pleasant moving in to the hotel, a place not too far from the Airport, a hotel which was very new, so new that it was still in process of being built! The Family moved along the long corridor and went up in the elevator. Miss Cleo was passing loud comments all the time, saying how much she liked the place and how glad she would be to be able to investigate all the scents and sights of the hotel. She is a great one for hotel life, she has experienced it in Fort Erie, Ontario, and she lived in a hotel in Prescott, Ontario, and then she spent quite a long time in the exceedingly pleasant hotel in Saint John, New Brunswick. So—Miss Cleopatra and Miss Tadalinka are very experienced hotel guests, and Cleo in particular has a virtue not possessed by many humans; when she knows that any act is unpopular with humans she doesn't do it again. She doesn't tear up furnishings, instead she uses her own scratch-pad, so there has never been a complaint against these little people in any hotel. They have always been invited to 'Come again and stay longer'.

The elevator glided to a halt, and we got out and moved in to the apartment—it is one of those hotels having a number of apartments to it—and Miss Cleo and Miss Tadalinka walked around inspecting everything and making loud comments about things. There were three rooms, and they went from one to the other walking over furniture, walking under beds— doing a job of investigation of which Sherlock Holmes himself would have approved!

Food too was an adventure for them. A different bellboy, different procedure, because the old man, being confined to a wheelchair, cannot manage in crowded dining rooms. There is always some clot who will trip over the chair, it happens time after time after time.

The lights of the hotel came on, and darkness began to settle in the basin-shaped valley which is British Columbia hemmed in by the Canadian Rockies. Above the mountain tops the light was still strong, although being streaked now with many colours. Down in the valley of Vancouver darkness, or rather dusk, was falling. All along the highway outside the window the greenish lights of the sodium lamps were glowing, warming up, or whatever it is they do, before lighting up to full brilliance. Traffic was streaming along into the city.

But the journey had been tiring. Three thousand miles of cramped accommodation with many, many problems and many, many worries was not really conducive to good health, not really conducive to peace of mind either. Soon the Family retired to bed—or no, not all the Family; Miss Cleo and Miss Tadalinka prowled about, sniffed under doors, and listened to all the strange sounds of hotel life as late revellers came and went, somewhat unsteadily at times.

In the morning the light came early. A beautifully fine sunny day, with not a trace of cloud, and, of course, here no snow. The climate was wonderful. The old man sat up in his bed and looked out of the window along the highway. Quite a collection of cars and the Police there so he picked up his binoculars to see what all the excitement was. Soon it dawned on him—the Mounties were operating one of their speed traps again! About twelve years before the old man had been to Vancouver and had decided against going there to live because of the utter fierceness of the Police. At that time he had been staying at the Hotel Vancouver, and looking out of a hotel window there was the sight of incessant police patrols putting tickets on parked cars, harassing drivers. And for two or three days he watched and saw that the police seemed to be extraordinarily savage in Vancouver. So for some twelve years he had decided against living in British Columbia. Now, looking out of the hotel window and watching the Mounties doing the same—and they did it day after day for as long as the old man looked—all the thoughts of the people came back to him, all the letters from people saying how difficult the police were in Vancouver. One woman wrote and said, 'You talk about the police of Montreal stopping you from going out, but just wait —if you ever come to Vancouver, they'll almost stop you from breathing!'

But now was the time for breakfast. Miss Cleo bustled

about making sure that everything was all right because she is a Siamese cat with a highly disciplined mind and she takes her responsibilities very very seriously indeed. She has to see that everyone is all right before she can settle down to her own food. Fat Cat Taddy, of course, who is nearly twice the weight of Miss Cleo, thinks of her own food first!

After breakfast the old man and one member of the Family went down into the hotel lobby to get a newspaper. Here right away he was recognized and, in spite of trying to snub the woman, she persisted. Immediately one person had recognized him, another did, so he turned back and wheeled along back to the hotel apartment thinking that there wasn't peace here either. He lay on the bed and read the newspapers while two other members of the Family went out apartment hunting; one went to all the addresses to which letters had been sent, the other went out on a 'free-lance' basis to try to find something.

The old man, Miss Cleo, and Miss Taddy all sat together in the hotel room as the long hours of the morning dragged by. Outside the traffic roared on incessant journeys to and from the city. Night workers coming off duty and returning to their homes in various parts of the Province, day workers thronging in to the city, for here distance doesn't seem to be any object. There is one taxi driver who drives about forty miles each way to get from his home to where he drives his taxi, and he still thinks he makes money!

Lunch-time came and passed, but soon after, within a short time of each other, the two missing members of the Family returned with a sorry tale for each to tell.

'Yes,' said one, 'they received your letters all right but they have a policy of not taking any pets so as you weren't going to rent from them they didn't bother to reply. They have nothing at all suitable because they will not take pets.'

The other had an equally sad tale: 'I went to all sorts of strange places trying to get somewhere but everywhere they say they will not take pets—get rid of your pets, they say, and then—yes—we will have you.'

The atmosphere—the climate, that is—of Vancouver is very nice indeed, it is a very pleasant place in which to live with beautiful parks, beautiful views, but for some extraordinary reason there seems to be a hatred of pets. Now, are these people inhumane, have they not reached a human standard yet, or why such a dislike of little people who often are a darn sight better and better behaved than the humans who deny them the right to living space.

The Family pondered the question, made enquiries, but always there was the same answer—no pets. One woman encountered by chance in a shopping mall said, 'Oh yes, it's right enough, here they won't take pets, I had to get rid of my cat before I could get an apartment anywhere. So I got rid of my cat and now I've got a one-bedroom apartment for which I pay a hundred and sixty dollars.'

No, the Family would not 'get rid of' Cleo or Taddy because these two are civilized, they are intelligent, and they are definite persons. So if necessary, the Family decided; if Vancouver is so inhospitable, then let us move somewhere else where the climate is perhaps not so good, but where the people are kinder.

The people of Vancouver do indeed seem to push themselves forward, they thrust themselves at others thinking they have a perfect right to accost anyone. The old man went to a shopping mall and three times in half an hour he was accosted most offensively by over-buoyant, over-enthusiastic people. But one of the gems of an encounter happened on the following day.

The old man was sitting in the wheelchair in a mall waiting for another member of the Family who was shopping. A young fellow came bounding along and more or less skidded to a stop in front of the old man: 'Hi!' he exclaimed. 'I know you, I've got a picture of you.'

'So have many people,' replied the old man somewhat sourly.

'Ah yes, but I've got a very special picture, a photograph of you with a friend of mine.'

By now the old man's interest was slightly aroused. What could be this wonderful photograph with a friend? So he said, 'A photograph of me with a friend of yours? Who is that, then?'

The young man smirked and looked wise. He said, 'Oh, I

131

know all about you. I've got a photograph of you and you've got your arm around the shoulders of a friend of mine. It was taken in England this year.'

The old man nearly fell out of his chair with amazement, and then he said, "But good gracious me, you just can't have! I wasn't in England this year. I haven't been to England for fifteen years.'

The young man looked at him, shook his head sadly and said, 'You can't be telling me the truth. What have you got to hide? I have a photograph of you taken in London in August 1972. You have your arm around the shoulders of a friend of mine.'

'But I'm telling you,' said the old man, 'I have not been in England for some fifteen years. You are mistaken somewhere.'

The young man shook his head with suspicion, then he said, 'You are Lobsang Rampa, aren't you?'

Naturally the old man admitted his identity, and the accoster shouted with triumph, 'Well then, you must have been in England in August 1972 because I've got your photograph to prove it.' And he turned and walked away shaking his head. The old man sat in his chair shaking his head!

But what a truly remarkable thing it is, all these imposters. The old man hadn't been in England for years, and he was not the type of person to get himself photographed with his arm around another person's shoulders! But there was worse—another person came along and said, 'Oh I saw you on television! I was in Baltimore a few weeks back and I saw you on the Something-Something Show.'

The old man said, 'Well, you couldn't have seen me there because I haven't been on a television show.'

The woman insisted, 'Oh, it was your name all right.' Then she thought a moment, 'But you did look different, I must admit. Perhaps you are more ill now, but it was someone with your name and I doubt if there are many people with the name of Tuesday Lobsang Rampa. No, it was you all right!' she exclaimed.

There was another case where someone wrote in and said they had just been watching a television show on Toronto television. She wrote and said, 'I have been just hearing from a man on television who said that you went to his house and you predicted that his wife was pregnant. Sure enough she was and they didn't know it! You said all about what the baby would be—and sure enough you were right. This man said he knows you well.' Marvels never cease because—no, I have not predicted that any person was pregnant. I have always thought that a person should be alert enough to know if they are going to have a child or not. It is not my place to tell them, particularly as I had no part in it! But it is really amazing how many mentally bankrupt people cannot do anything themselves so they just have to ape someone else who has some sort of a name. Recently there has been quite an upsurge in people pretending that they are me or pretending that I am a bosom friend of theirs, etc., etc.

When I was in Prescott I had a letter from a woman who lived in Montreal. She wrote to me calling me 'husband', and as I read on I became more and more amazed because her letter gave me to understand that I was the father of her child. I had apparently—strictly according to her—been to visit her in the astral and—er, done what has to be done to produce that required effect. So the woman thought that I was the astral father of her yet unborn son. Well, it was news to me! But I am reminded of that because now within the past few weeks I have had a letter from a woman in England who again thinks that I am the father of her child although I am about six thousand miles away from her, and I haven't been to England for fifteen years. Either I have tremendous physical attributes or things are rather long delayed, aren't they. However, poor sick minds can imagine anything I suppose. But that is just put in to show you what sort of people sometimes bother an unfortunate author. I suppose a Roman Catholic priest who is unmarried and has the title of 'Father' feels something the same as I do about it. He is unmarried, he is called 'Father' even though he has probably never even thought of 'doing his stuff'.

But the search had to be continued. How to find a place to live? How to manage? Hotel bills mount up and to stay as a guest in an hotel for too long—well, one has to have the resources of a Rockefeller to bear that. Even Howard Hughes seems to have to move from hotel to hotel!

More enquiries were made, more letters were written. A letter was written to one of those places that guarantee to find suitable accommodation. A reply came back very swiftly: 'Oh, I know you, Dr. Rampa, I do so want to meet you. I cannot find you any accommodation because of your pets, but I do want to come and meet you.'

Eventually the Family moved further downtown in the hope of being nearer the scene of things, in the hope that personal contacts would enable them to find accommodation. They moved downtown to yet another hotel which would, at least for the time being, take the cats.

It seemed that things would be slow, so the typewriter was unpacked and once again a start was made on *Candlelight*. Having made a start on *Candlelight* then surely we should go back to discussing these problems, these questions, which seem to perplex so many people.

CHAPTER EIGHT

The old man was sitting before the eternal pile of letters. Suddenly he picked one up and there was the rustle of paper, then he started to chuckle: 'Hey,' he called out, 'listen to this; this is in a letter which I have just opened.'

He read out from the letter, 'There was one of these charter flights going from Los Angeles to London, England. A group of people were going to have a tour of the historic places of London and of England. The plane arrived in England and the tour began. All the people got into one of the chartered buses and drove off to a place called Runymede, one of the historic places of the world not just of England, a place where liberty started centuries ago.

'The Guide stood up before the crowd of American tourists with their Bermuda shorts and their cameras and their owlish eyes behind their great glasses, and he said, "And here, ladies and gentlemen, is a truly historic spot. This is an important place; 1215 Magna Carta was signed here." One fat floosey looked at her watch and snorted with annoyance: "Too bad! We missed it by twenty minutes." '

But it is such a short step from mirth to melancholy. Here is a person who is most concerned about—death.

'You write a lot about death and about the joys in it for those who escape from the difficulties of the Earth, but you never say anything of help to us who are left here. How about telling us something in the book you are writing about grief and what we can do? It's all right for those who have passed over, but it's not so all right for those of us who are left. So how about saying a bit about grief?'

Very well, that's fair enough: Death and grief are so grossly

135

misunderstood, misrepresented. Just about everyone in existence has had grief, the loss of a loved child, the loss of a loved parent or partner. Grief is a terrible thing indeed and if one sits hard on one's emotions it can do definite damage. People should understand that the system approved by present-day society is not always the best. The old Chinese, for instance, used to laugh (pseudo) heartily as they told of the death of a loved one. The old Chinese simply could not face the thought of showing their emotion, showing the emotion of grief, to the world and so they put on a wholly artificial levity about the matter.

There is no way of terminating the pain which a loss causes us, no way of ending the grief. Only time can do that. Time heals all, time will terminate the pain of grief, time will terminate the troubles of this turbulent Earth, time will end life itself.

One of the biggest curses of modern-day life is the attitude of the undertakers and funeral home people because they, no doubt for reasons of business, try to pretend that one's 'loved one' is not dead but merely sleeps. These undertakers paint the dead faces, they wave the dead hair, they prop up the dead body as if simulating a person who is drowsing on a cushion of satin.

It seems to be a universal conspiracy in present day life to conceal grief as if there is something shockingly shameful in showing emotion at a loss.

A person who goes on a long journey to the other side of the world, for instance—well, there is always the possibility of the person coming back. But when a person is dead then that person has gone from this Earth and it is highly improbable that they will come back. Often grief is tinged with definite hostility, hostility that a person has died and left one. Now, just think about that and, irrational though it seems, it is true—there is some sort of sub-conscious hostility towards a dead person. Often, too, there is a feeling of guilt. Could we have done more for the suffering person? Could we have in any way saved the life? Could we have eased the suffering? Well, if a person 'puts us in the wrong' we often resent that person so when a death occurs there is much 'soul-searching'—who is to blame, what more could have been done, or 'how could he have done this thing to me, how could he have gone out of my life'?

Undertakers go to fantastic lengths to pretend that the corpse is just a sleeping body. They falsify values, and, in my opinion, it is very wrong indeed to shove a body in some unnatural attitude—unnatural for death, that is—and pretend that he or she is just sleeping. We should have a new concept of death. Nations should spend money investigating death and teaching people that grief is natural, grief is normal, grief is a safety valve enabling one's bottled emotions to be harmlessly drained away.

Great men like Winston Churchill were not afraid to shed tears when the occasion warranted it. Winston Churchill, it is said, could shed tears of emotion and tears of grief, and he was a better man for it.

Now you ask what could be done to help a person suffering grief through the loss of a partner or relative—let us not have any of this hypocrisy about 'a loved one' because often young people find a great relief in the loss or death of an old tiresome parent. They feel ashamed of their relief and so they rant on about 'loved one'.

The first thing to do is to face that death has occurred, to face that things are now different. There will be red tape, interfering officials will want all sorts of papers signed. Heartless officials of the country will want their own share of whatever legacy is left. One can help a lot by listening to the person who has been bereaved, listen and let the grieving person talk, let the person talk out his or her sorrows, let him or her discuss the past. In this way guilt will be drained off, grief will be drained off and the one who has died will be freer.

It is quite essential that a person be helped to get over grief, it doesn't do to let a person stay alone grieving, mourning with a hard straight face showing nothing to the outside world because such grief bottled up inside one appears somewhere. It is like a steam boiler—you can't screw down the safety valve and keep on putting on the heat, something will burst eventually. A person who is overcome with grief which is kept bottled up will later suffer from ulcers or severe bowel trouble, or it can even start arthritis. In extreme cases—and I have two such neighbours not too far away from me—schizophrenia can occur. A young woman, for instance, who appears to have everything, who appears to be fairly balanced, can suddenly be struck down by the death of a relative, she becomes mentally deranged, she wanders about brooding, sullen, and dirty. These things happen, but they would not happen if there was more understanding of the nature of grief, it would not happen if neighbours would help by letting the person talk, by keeping silent themselves except for sympathetic noises at the appropriate times.

How many times do you hear a bereaved person say, 'If only I had acted differently he would be with us today.' There are other cases where a bereaved person will rant at the dead person, ranting on about *why* did he die and leave me, *what* am I going to do now?

One of the worst features of the funeral service is the eulogy where someone speaks a whole lot of hogwash about the bereaved. No one who has ever died is bad, it seems. People search around for someone who can tell a whole lot of lies saying how good the dead person was and what a dreadful loss it will be to the community. But that is bad, you know, it makes a bereaved person think that he or she has lost something far, far greater than is really the case.

There are often cases where a husband loses his wife, perhaps in childbirth. The man, now a father, has undisguised hostility for the poor innocent baby who in being born quite inadvertently caused the death of the mother. So there is a father ruined and a baby ruined right at the start. If people would only clear up their conceptions about things.

Now grief—what is it? Often it is selfishness. It is often opposition to any change. People do not like a change which is permanent, and so when death occurs—well, that is permanent, that is a considerable change, and resentment and hostility occur.

What you should do is this; help a person who is bereaved by encouraging that person to talk, and if the person weeps so much the better. In weeping the emotions are released and there is then no risk of one's sanity. You can talk gently but

138

firmly to the person, telling them to weep, telling them not to bottle up their emotions, telling them that—yes, they have had a terrible loss but soon they too will be moving to the other side of the curtain which divides the dead of this world from the living of the next world. And if you are a good psychologist—the best psychologists come from the homes and not from the offices of so-called professional men—you can do a lot to help those who need your help.

I do want to mention here that, whereas people should be encouraged to give vent to grief in order to 'get it out of their system', they should not be encouraged to persist in grief because such is merely grieving for their own loss and not genuine grief, it is self-pity and such is not to be encouraged.

While on this subject here is another letter which surely does apply to the present; 'A most shocking thing occurred when my father was dying. My young daughter just 18 years of age lay down on a couch and—do you know?—*she fell sound asleep when my father was dying.* I can never forgive her for that!'

But, you know, we must remember that there are certain people who are 'helpers of those passing over'. These persons, it doesn't matter what age they are, it doesn't matter what class they are, but these persons have an ability to help a person over into the next life in much the same way as a midwife has the ability to help a baby to become born and separated from its mother. The midwife has to stay wide awake, but the 'helper' has to appear to go to sleep because the astral form has to emerge from the body. Hence, in this case, the young daughter did not thoughtlessly 'fall asleep'. Instead she had the ability to leave her body and help her grandfather to enter his new life.

There are so many things that could be said on the matter of death. For example, in the days of Atlantis and Lemuria there were always bodies kept in cool chambers, dead bodies, or apparently dead bodies. These were 'entity-less' bodies which were kept so that the Gardeners of the Earth could at any time take over a body and appear among humans as a human. These were the first examples of 'time travel' because the Gardeners of the Earth, who know all and can do all, have to travel to different worlds and mix with different entities, and so, as stated, they do keep certain bodies which can be entered by arrangement. This is not necessarily the same as transmigration because in the latter an entity takes over a body—by special arrangement and special permission, of course—and remains in that body for the rest of its life on Earth. But the Gardeners of the Earth could take over a body, go anywhere for a time, and then leave the body just the same as a person can rent a car, do a journey, and then return the car to the renters. Possibly we ought to start up a travel service on those lines!

Now, let us say a few words about getting old. It is a thoroughly obnoxious practice which affects us all, no matter how much we try to disguise that unpleasant fact, no matter how much powder and paint we put on, no matter how much we try to tell ourselves otherwise, there comes a time when in the morning you find your joints are creaking a bit, you find you don't get up as easily as you did. So you then reach the inescapable conclusion that you are getting old.

When people are getttng old or, rather, when they have become old, they do seem to go to pieces rather quickly, but that is natural, isn't it? Whatever you say about it, people are just flowers of the Overself! Flowers are merely devices to draw attention to the seeds, and people, then, are just the flowers which have the seeds to reproduce other members of a species or a race. A woman is supposed to be attractive to the male so that in the union which follows certain acts occur which enable the race to be propagated and so to continue. After all, men and women are here for a purpose, to continue the race so that all the time people are learning and learning. But according to the basic law of Nature when reproduction is no longer possible because of deterioration caused by age, then there is no longer any real need for the life to continue. When people have gone beyond the age at which they can contribute towards producing other humans, then on the purely material plane they have finished.

In the old days when the race of Man was young, people lived to be thirty or forty years of age, and then when they could no longer sire or bear children they died off. It was

140

much the same as flowers; you get a plant, eventually on the plant flowers bloom and seeds are within the flower. After a time the flower withers and falls off, so that is the end of that flower. It has done its task in having the seeds and making the seeds available. When that task is ended, the reason for the existence of the flower also has ended. Humans used to be more like that.

But science, so-called, has prolonged the life span perhaps two or three times as much as was normal in the early days of the race. But people still chase around trying to give an illusion of youth because they have a racial memory that without the ability to reproduce they are no longer of use, and so they seek a false youth in which they are trying to persuade others that—yes—I can still sire or bear children, and that, they claim, is an excuse or reason for going on living. We see this particularly in the life story of Hollywood idols. A fellow claims that he is the 'biggest sirer of children' in existence. Or some crummy looking film actress with probably surgically increased bust uplift claims that she is the best sex symbol ever. Phooey! It's the mind and the soul that matter, not the lumps of meat which clothe the bony framework.

In the oldest races people used to die young except for a very few old people who were deliberately left there by the Gardeners of the Earth to teach and to pass on knowledge of a far more than normal lifetime. But this present day craze with women getting themselves done up like something they never were—well, that is a matter of self-justification which means that they still want to compete on the field (or should it be bed?) of sex. If people would only 'be themselves' and 'act their age' they would be far happier. There would be less nervous troubles, there would be less hostility from other age groups.

But, sad though it seems, it may even be that the Gardeners of the Earth are to blame for the horrible state to which mankind has descended. When a garden—no matter how wonderful that garden be—is neglected for too long through the absence of its gardener then the garden degenerates, everything 'goes to pot'. Humans sure have gone there fast, humans are in a great state of confusion about their origin. They don't know

141

why they should consider material things and metaphysical things. They don't know where things fit in. They see a human body but they don't see the soul, so they are more inclined to place credence on the purely physical human body. And yet, humans pray to or revere a Trinity which through long years of Christian usage is known as Father, Son, and Holy Ghost. Actually, the Trinity is the Overself which is the Holy Ghost, the astral form which is the intermediary, and then the third which is the purely physical body on the Earth.

The physical body on the Earth is the labourer, the one who does hard things to learn hard lessons which the more intangible Overself could not endure. You can say, in a similar way, that an uncouth savage could endure more torture than a highly refined gentlewoman. So the physical torture would be on the lowest plane, but the highly refined gentlewoman would be able to withstand far more mental shocks than would the savage. Humans should remember that they are basically three entities, the physical which is the earth body, the astral, and the Overself. Actually, there are nine different sheaths from the physical to the astral, but that does not matter for now because they are in different dimensions and when one is trying to discuss things in a three dimensional category it is not easily possible to discuss things of a nine dimensional existence.

And—to confuse you thoroughly—on other planes of existence there are more than the nine sheaths. You can add a few noughts if you have ever been there. I have!

A Christian parson who is very anxious that his name will not be mentioned writes to me, in fact he is so anxious that his name will not be mentioned—that he doesn't give any! Unfortunately for him he used a piece of his own headed paper and in a moment of forgetfulness wrote on the obverse, or, if you like it simple, he wrote on the side which had no address. The other side carried his name and address! Never mind, I won't give his name nor his address, but I will tell you this; many people of religious persuasion write to me, bishops write to me, a cardinal has been in correspondence with me and, incidentally, thoroughly, thoroughly approving of my work. A pity I can't get him to give a statement to the Press, eh? And then there is another gentleman of 'the Cloth' who is a Jesuit and a very high professor indeed of that Order. He teaches other Jesuits of 'high degree'. All these people approve of my work, all these people write to me giving their names and addresses quite safe in the knowledge that I never disclose names and addresses except at the request of, or with the permission of, the person so quoted. Not everyone wants publicity. I don't for one!

But back to our bashful priest; he writes me a nice letter exclaiming in horror and amazement that people cannot believe my books. He tells me that the Catholic Church teach their adherents that at death the Christian—the Catholic Christian—leaves the physical body and then God gives them a spirit one. I gather that after they all sing Hallelujah together and play a few harps and flap about the astral countryside. Well, okay, everyone to their own Belief, but in substance this is only the same as what I have been writing about. Of course people leave the physical body and then they are not given a spirit body because they already have it—the astral body.

Now, it is really unfortunate that this Respected Reverend thinks that he is anonymous because I would have liked to have written to him and told him that—no, people do not disbelieve my books. I think during the last sixteen years that I have not had more than four or five really offensive letters, letters expressing doubt, etc. I have kept those in my—what shall I call it?—Black Museum. But these are only the rantings of diseased minds. One person told me that God was going to strike me down dead, but if I would send her a sum of money she would see that God wouldn't strike me down dead. Well, I didn't send any money and I am still here.

Another 'lady' wrote to me highly incensed because I wrote about back street healers and all that sort of thing. She told me of the wonders she had accomplished, how she cured cancer, and I believe (it is too much trouble to look up!) that she almost raised the dead. But now she wrote to me full of fury because people read my books and the cash customers had fallen off sharply. She accused me of ruining her income. Amusing, eh?

143

I had another letter from a gentleman of colour who wrote on behalf of himself and a friend. They said they would like to come and see me because they wanted both to become doctors, so they wrote to me and asked if I would send them First Class air fares and provide them with an adequate sum of money so they could look around a bit in the U.S.A. and decide where they would like to live. The writer then went on to tell me that when they had decided where they would like to live I could pay for the training of the two and all their living expenses for about five years—'longer', wrote one, 'if we should decide to specialize'. Of course they made it very clear that they would never be able to pay me back, but they gave me an absolute assurance that they would pray for me every day of my life.

Naturally enough I was touched to think of these gentlemen of colour so heartily praying for me if I would give them thousands and thousands of pounds just for love of gentlemen of colour, but I wasn't touched enough to part with a penny. Nowadays I have to look at both sides of the penny, and I wish I was skilled in some of the arts known as splitting a note in two! Unfortunately in Canada, as well as in other countries of the world, the Government do not like people to print their own money or make their own money; the Government likes to keep a monopoly on that subject although they look with great repugnance on other people who have a monopoly in anything. So there it is, the gentlemen of colour go untrained, and I go with virgin purity at least so far as counterfeiting is concerned.

Now we've got to get on with some of these questions. You keep distracting me, you know! Of course it is you who distracts me because if you didn't keep on sending in these letters to me I shouldn't be side-tracked by some of the curious comments you sometimes make. But, anyway, back to these questions:

A lady from India is most puzzled; she writes: 'The caul, which is a membrane which sometimes encloses a baby at birth, has it got any metaphysical or psychic significance to that individual?'

No, it doesn't mean a thing. It doesn't mean any more than some people being born with black hair, some people being born with—whatever you call it—blonde hair, the ginger stuff.

A caul is just something peculiar to that person and it does not in any way increase one's psychic ability or spiritual power. Some people think otherwise, but it is really just an old wives' tale as some people believe it is bad luck to have a black cat cross one's path at midnight on a moonless night—I don't know how they would see that black cat, though, do you? Others think that it is good fortune to have the aforementioned cat cross one's path under the aforementioned conditions. So there it is, I suggest you take the penny which I mentioned previously and decide which way you want to believe, and then toss up the penny to see if you are right or wrong. I state that a caul doesn't mean a thing.

Now here is a question: 'Most causes which have influence upon us physically, that is, cancer, poverty, blindness, etc., have some form of fund to which one can contribute in order to help in all aspects of the problem in question. Is it possible to set up such a fund which could help causes such as yours?'

Oh ho, my dear madam, that is a thing loaded with atom bomb material! The next thing we should find, if such a thing were done, is that the Press would start up saying that I was exploiting the public or defrauding people or some similar rot.

Some time ago it was suggested that I start up as a Foundation (no, not the type of foundation worn by women but the benevolent kind), but I am not at all keen on that because so many 'cults' do have such a Foundation which enables them to set up some sort of stunt where they do not pay income tax on money received, but which does enable them to pay very high salaries to themselves, to each other, for 'specialist services', whatever that means. I am honest, and regrettably honest enough to have an instinctive abhorrence of these Foundations. So many of them are not what they purport to be.

I always take the view that if a person is really anxious to help in the matter of research into the aura or into the other matters in which I am desperately interested, then they can always help with a donation if they want to, but that must be their own decision.

Now, here is something which is going to rock you on your heels; this question is—wait a minute, let's get it straight— 'On the subject of Tai Chi, in *Wisdom of the Ancients* you said that the wise men of China used Tai Chi to indicate that to which we return upon leaving this world. It is the ultimate or the end of all things incarnate. It is reunion with one's Overself and the state which upon Earth can only be likened to bliss. Do you think you can expand on this? For example, has the Tai Chi got any light for us today, and what of its origin?'

But that is all that I have been telling you about in thirteen books! When we leave this Earth we are a step nearer 'Home'. Each step up from plane to plane brings increases in joy or what the questioner calls 'bliss'. On each low stage of evolution we have to work hard with relatively slight reward, but the higher we go the greater our responsibilities, the less the physical work, and the higher the aspirations possible to us. So that on this Earth, for example, we can work with pick and shovel 'to the Glory of God'. There is nothing shameful in hard work. But you would not get the same remuneration as the President of the Company employing you. You would get hard work and lower pay, but low responsibility, while the poor fellow sitting in his padded chair (I almost said 'padded cell'!) gets high pay, low physical work, and enough responsibility to give him ulcers. Well, the higher you go the less physical work you do, but the greater enjoyment you derive from doing a job well, the greater pleasure you get from being in the service of others. And the higher we go—well, when we get to the ninth plane of existence, for instance, we get in a state of bliss which would be quite incomprehensible in three dimensional terms. It is like—dare I mention love?—On Earth through the onset of the Christian inhibitory practises love is all mixed up with what is also known as sex, and here sex is regarded as something unspeakable, it is regarded as 'dirty'. So it is quite useless to try to explain to a person bogged down in imagined filth what love and sex are like on the ninth dimension. There are no terms to describe it, and yet you have to have such a union of highly evolved souls before you can know what joy, bliss, rapture, happiness, and all the rest of it really mean.

'Has the Tai Chi got any light for us today?' Well, we are in the Age of Kali, we are in the descending stroke of the pendulum, and things are going to get a lot worse before they get a lot better. We are going down into the depths. When we reach the lowest point then we shall start going up again until we reach what is, in effect, a state of rapture upon this Earth. Of course you and I won't be here then. We shall have passed to our just reward centuries before that time. But we can assure our place on the upward path if we at all times remember—Do unto others as you would have them do unto you, and then you will be out of the Age of Kali and on the way of Tai Chi.

We are going up in the world once again; a countess sends me a bunch of questions. Do you want some questions from a countess? All right, here is the first one:

'When a new world is created the inhabitants for this world are also created to fit the living conditions. Are their souls also newly created or are they already created and existing at that time?'

When a new world is created the entities are already existing. Think of it like this:

New York is overcrowded, there are far too many people there so there could be a shortage of food, a shortage of electricity, a shortage of water, and a shortage of everything in fact. So a fresh satellite, town, city, or dormitory town is set up somewhere within reach, let us say West Chester, for example. A load of people go to West Chester and set up stores and all the rest of it. In effect that is a new world, so when we get a new world created it means that one of the old worlds is overcrowded or it is due for disintegration. You see, the Sun, after all, is just an atomic pile and though it might seem millions of years old to us yet it is just the twinkling of an eye in certain other times.

You find that difficult to comprehend? Take a match in your hand and think of that as in dead space, it is just a dead lump. Then strike it on the side of the match box and it will burst into flames. All sorts of small particles will be emitted and thrown out from the flaming surface. They, being much smaller, will cool very much more rapidly and yet they will, so long as they are in close proximity to the match flame, be warmed. But that explosion of the match bursting into flame is only a second or two, isn't it. Perhaps it is not even that long.

147

but just think of that sun giving birth to little planets which are pieces thrown off, and those planets having the start of life, life itself. And then the decay of life as the flame of the central sun (the match head) has a diminishing flame and then becomes a burnt out husk. That is how worlds go on. To us here on these particles, or rather, on one particular particle, it seems that the worlds exist for millions of years, but to people looking from afar it is just like a match head bursting into sudden flame, flaring, and expiring.

Question Two: 'If these souls are newly created, how far does the multiplication go? How much room do we have? Where does it end?'

We are up against relativity here. Actually space is limitless. We are not dealing with just a three dimensional thing but with things of all dimensions and things of no dimensions. On Earth we are limited to certain dimensions, for example, I am in a room. The room has four sides, it has a roof (fortunately!), and it has a floor. When I am in this room and the door is shut I cannot go out without opening the door, but if a person of the fourth dimension, who we would call a ghost, wanted to come in—well, there would be no problem because the molecules of the wall here would be so tenuous to a ghost that he would simply drift through without any problems at all. It is something like ice which is a hard solid substance. People living on a world of ice would have no conception of what their souls would be like, but let us 'kill' some ice, let us alter its rate of vibration because when a thing dies its rate of vibration alters. This ice, then, that we are going to 'kill' turns into water. It is a completely different sort of substance from ice. The water flows, it can take up the shape of the receptacle which retains it. But we want to find the 'soul of ice' so let us heat up the water and thereby increase its vibration, and then we get steam, a gas. So if you think of a body—a human body—as being represented by ice, then you can readily appreciate that the next stage up when the ice turns to water is when we get out of the body and get into the astral world and we flow about. Beyond that—well, we go from the water stage up into the water vapour stage, up into the gas stage. So you could not push a piece of ice through an apparently solid sub-

148

stance such as a piece of blotting paper, but you could push water through. Even better, you could blow steam all the way through easily.

You can see, though, that the molecules of ice, the molecules of water, and the molecules of steam are different. They get more and more dispersed as one goes up. We get the same thing with the body and the soul of Man.

Question Three: 'We were taught that our Maker is a one God. Is really just one Entity at the head of all creation, or is it a governing group at the head of our "All"?'

You really do ask the stickiest of questions in this one about God. You ask is it really one Entity at the head of all creation. Look at it like this; you are a human and presumably you have a head, feet, arms, and a few other bits stuck on your body at strategic points. All this makes *you*—just one of you—and your hands, your feet, your knees, your—*everything*—goes to form that one, and all those parts are dependent upon each other. Of course you could do without a hand or without a leg, but you couldn't do without a head although most people seem to try to nowadays. But 'God' is that entity which comprises the whole of the Universes and there are billions of them, and each Universe and part of a Universe is an essential part of the basic 'God'.

Question Four: 'Will our souls live forever after we will graduate from this world? After so many lives we will go to better places, you have me convinced of that fact. How many worlds will we graduate to and where will we end?'

Yes, our 'souls' will live as long as 'God' lives because our souls, our Overselves, etc., are just part of the fabric of God. If you stick a pin in yourself and withdraw it from your quivering body it may appear that the pin is quite clean, bare of everything, but if you stick it in the field of a very powerful microscope you may find one lonely molecule waving at you through the electronic magnifier. Well, that one lonely molecule can be just as you are to 'God'.

Question Five: 'I was brought up a Catholic and went to school in a convent. We were taught very little about the years Jesus had disappeared. Was He really in Asia learning during that time? So many books say so many different things about

149

the subject. If He spent all these years in Asia He must have liked what he learned. Of course my entire conception of Him has changed since I became really more religious which has nothing to do with a particular religion. You will hear from me again—soon.'

Now, I wonder if that last statement, 'You will hear from me again—soon' was a promise or a threat. I must think about it, but anyway——

Yes, Jesus the man wandered abroad in the Wilderness, the Wilderness being that part of the world which was not His immediate and familiar vicinity or the vicinity of His birth. Jesus went throughout India, throughout China, and into Tibet, and much of the original Christian religion is actually a conglomeration of Eastern religions which have been hashed up, worked over, and tailored to fit what is, in effect, a Western mentality.

Most certainly Jesus liked what He found in the East because after, according to the Press report which I have already given you, He went to Japan instead of being crucified!

After Jesus the man came back from His travels, He went again into a distant place where He would not be bothered by onlookers, and there He left His physical body and went on to other places. His body was taken over by another entity from space as had previously been arranged. So Jesus the man departed His body and the spirit of Christ took over and became 'the Christ'. That, then, is transmigration and nothing else.

So many people seem to find difficulty in comprehending this matter of transmigration, but Christ taught it. Christ taught reincarnation also, and if people would read the Bible with an open mind they would understand all these things. They should also take into consideration the definite fact that the Bible now is not as it was originally nor how it was intended to be. The Bible has been translated, re-translated, mis-translated, re-hashed, and thousands of different editions brought out. Sometimes the head of a Church will say that such a thing cannot be taught any more. Then he will scratch his own head and bring out something else which should be taught. The Bible should be looked upon as a general statement of policy rather than a blow by blow, round by round account of what happened. It is quite a good book but you have to use common sense in reading a book which is so old and which is so different in concept to that which originally was planned.

CHAPTER NINE

'Hey!' screamed the words from the letter. 'How is it that you, who have been doing aura work for so long, never get a good write-up in the Press?'

The old man thoughtfully pulled out a newspaper cutting which was stuck in the big envelope. It was from some paper called 'The National Enquirer' dated September 24th, 1972. It seemed that some fellow was falling over backwards—frontwards as well—to praise up the Russians and their efforts in aura research.

It purports to say that plants 'know' when the weather is going to change. Well, of course they do. I have been saying that for years.

It also says 'the plain fact is that the Soviets are years ahead of the U.S. in research on E.S.P., in the fields of mind over matter, telepathy, etc., that we may never catch up.'

And—'the astounding colour movies of the human aura the Russians have made show how far they have already gone——!'

But, yet, I have been doing things like this for years. Anyway, I have had all the details about this fellow and the article before, and I wrote to him sending some of my books, telling him the truth as I have been informed of it; the Russians were greatly impressed with *You—Forever* and it sparked considerable research in Russia. The Russians have bought quite a lot of books and they have made good use of the hints, etc., which I have given.

Yes, yes, it's just fine that the Russians are making progress, but why not give a little credit here as well? It does seem to me that people just go crazy with joy and delight if the Communists of Russia copy someone else and find that it works, but now that I am a Canadian citizen I find that a prophet is without honour in his own country! I find my books are being quoted and quoted and misquoted with never a trace of acknowledgment to me—the author—but I suppose that is the way of life.

There is another book eulogizing Russian 'science' and the remarks above also apply to that book. I sent some details to the authors of the book, but again they did not even have the common courtesy to reply, not even the courtesy to say 'thank you'. I have come to the conclusion that I must be some sort of a nut for answering people's letters and saying 'thank you' if they send me a cutting or something. People have told me that, by the way—that I am a nut for bothering with so many people. Never mind, it might help someone. But I do want to put on record that the Russians do not have a monopoly on aura research. The Russians do seem to have a monopoly of finance to help research and without money to buy equipment—well, many a promising invention has been still-born. That is what I am finding now. There is a 'telephone to heaven' and a good aura camera, because the stuff the Russians are doing so far is not the true aura but the sub-etheric auric sheath. They haven't got down to the real thing yet, but they might in time!

Another letter asks 'Is it true that most of the great leaders of the world were tradesmen, and if so—why?'

Well, yes, you can say that. You can say that most of the great leaders of the world started from what are called 'humble origins' and there is a special reason for that. It is thought by the Gardeners of the Earth that those who come here to help humanity must be in touch with the majority of humans, and if a man comes as a king then in the normal course of events he is only in contact with those of kingly, princely, or ducal status.

Jesus was the son of a carpenter. Possibly He took a swipe or two with carpentry tools himself, we never hear that He was a carpenter but only the son of a carpenter. Mohammed, who was one of the great people, was an Arab tradesman, and then at the age of forty he began to have all sorts of messages and 'conversations with Messengers'. The content of the Messengers' instructions led him to organize the Moslem religion, and write the Koran.

Moses—well, he was just a homeless waif who had the luck —good or bad—to be picked up by a princess, but the point is that he was still a homeless waif who had the 'common touch'.

Gautama, of course, was a Prince, that is he started off a Prince. But he soon found that as a Prince he was not in touch with the common people, so he renounced his princely caste and went into the wilderness away from his bunch of wives who made quite a commotion about being left husbandless, but in spite of great efforts to persuade him to change his mind Gautama went into the wilderness as a poor and humble man and became 'the Buddha', the Founder of Buddhism. He had to renounce his high estate and relinquish his wealth before he could indeed get in touch with the ordinary people who most needed help.

Here is a question which I frankly do not quite understand. The question is: 'Is there an absolute possibly existing somewhere in the seventh through the ninth dimensions?'

Now, I do not understand that one because what is 'an absolute'? I wonder if the person who writes means a God, and if that is the case, well, the answer is No. Even the Manus go up much higher than the ninth dimension. The Manus that one can experience looking after this world, for example, they are the puppets of an Overself Manu.

Now here is a question for you: 'Are there less and less laws governing an entity the higher up on the evolutionary scale he goes?'

Yes, basically that is so. The laws are actually made to control the masses, and often a law which is most beneficial to a mass of people is horribly unjust to some poor wretched individual. But laws cannot be made to suit each and every individual. A law has to be formulated so that it may embrace the great majority of people coming within its dictum.

If you had read the 1972 tax forms you would know what I mean! The instructions about this wretched form are so abstruse that I honestly can't make any sense at all out of it, and I imagine that there are many more like me. But back to our question; the higher a person evolves the less the need for

154

stereotyped laws to control his behaviour because when he reaches a high enough position he knows instinctively what he should do and what he should not do, and he doesn't need the disservices of law makers to tie him up in red tape and so ruin whatever it is he is trying to do.

A question: 'Does it become proportionally easier to evolve the higher the plane of evolvement?'

Well, that is relative, you know. You have to keep in mind that the higher you go the greater the distance that you can fall, but I can only answer this question by returning to the classroom.

If one has a child at school studying then he is trained to study, trained to remember, trained to absorb information. If the child then leaves school and takes some ordinary job such as an office boy or something, then he lapses and he gets out of the habit of studying so that if after a few years he has to study something he finds the process remarkably difficult and painful.

If a child is studying and continues to study, up and up through high school, through university, perhaps on to medical or law school, then the child, now young adult, is trained in studying and he finds it easier and easier to study as he studies more and more. So you could say a person who is consciously, continually evolving—and not backsliding—can evolve more easily than those who are 'dragging their feet'. But if the person does make a mistake and stops his own evolution, then he may go in reverse, he may go the wrong way and lose much of his evolution, so then he has to come back and relearn his lessons. By that time he will find they are much harder.

A question is: 'Do all human entities possess an astral body?'

Oh definitely they do, everything does, not just humans but all animals, even rocks. Everything vibrates. There is no such thing as a stationary object in existence, such a thing is impossible. Every single article that there is anywhere is in a state of constant molecular motion. You might look at a mountain and think it is just a stupid lump of rock stuck in the middle of a landscape to prevent you from seeing what is at the other side. But it is not like that; it is a great mass of

155

vibrating molecules, and the action of all these molecules vibrating together is to set up a form of electric field which gives an astral body and also an aura. So the answer is—yes, everything has an astral body, everything has an aura.

Sometimes I get taken to task, although, I must admit, in the kindest ways, for apparently repeating myself. I am told that I tell the same thing two or three times in two or three ways, but then I get a letter from a person who tells me that he or she is very grateful that I have repeated myself because at last I have got through and made a point. The first and second attempts at explaining weren't successful, the third was. But now I've got a question: 'Would you please again explain how to control one's mind, how to direct thought?'

Now I have already dealt with that quite a lot, but I have definitely been asked to repeat it, so all you people who do not like repetition—*read on* because you might just learn something!

We have to remember that we are only one-tenth conscious, and the real source of knowledge, the real source of action, is the sub-conscious. But the sub-conscious is like a lazy old man who wants to sit and smoke a pipe all day and not do anything. He knows he is the custodian of great knowledge, etc., but he doesn't want to part with any of it, he doesn't want to move. So you have to get through to him to galvanize him into action.

If you want to direct thought or control your mind, then you have to know what you want because it is useless to seek a thing unless you know what you are seeking, otherwise if you do not know what you are seeking you won't know when you have found it, will you?

Let us suppose you want to learn something; well, you sit down somewhere where it is quiet and you think of the matter which you desire to study. Perhaps you are afraid your memory will fail you or something, but anyway you think of the matter you desire to study. Tell your sub-conscious what you want to do, tell your sub-conscious why you want to do it, say what benefits will be derived from learning such a matter. You have to get it over to your sub-conscious that you and 'George' or 'Georgina' are all part of the same firm so what harms one

156

harms the other, what benefits one benefits the other. So you have to think about the thing you want to do, you have to think about it directly, you have to think all around it, you have to think of all the advantages. Then you have actually to visualize yourself studying the subject or possessing the object, and if you make a real campaign about it—do it perhaps three times in succession—the sub-conscious may be roused and will then help you to attain that which you desire.

You have to go in for visualization. Now, visualization is not imagination. Imagination is something which can be indulged in on the imaginary basis only. No amount of imagination, for instance, would enable you to jump over a thirty-storey building. You might be able to do it in your imagination and then you would be something like Buck Rogers, wouldn't you? But such a jump—over a thirty-storey building—is beyond the laws of physical nature so it is imagination only, and many people waste time imagining that which is impossible.

Visualization, on the contrary, is something which is entirely possible because it is entirely in keeping with normal physical laws. As an illustration, suppose you want to buy a boat, then if you visualize yourself suddenly coming into possession of a large sum of money and going to the place where they sell boats, looking over them, and finally deciding on such a boat then you may find that your visualizations bear fruit. It is a fact that if the conditions are right anything you visualize you can have—in time. It may not be just at the moment you want it, but you will get it—if you visualize things properly.

You have to sit down comfortably. You have to cross your ankles and clasp your hands in front of you. Then you put out a very strong thought to your sub-conscious, calling him or her by the private name which I suggested earlier in this book. You tell your sub-conscious three times, 'Attention! Attention! Attention!' Then you say, 'Look into my mind now.' You repeat that three times, and then you think very definitely, very clearly on the matter for which you desire the co-operation of your sub-conscious. Let us get back to pendulums.

You want your pendulum to tell you where such-and-such a thing is, so it might be a lump of gold and in that case you will tune your pendulum for a lump of gold (I told you how to do

157

that earlier in this book). Then you will visualize yourself holding the pendulum by its cord and the swing indicating gold. You will pick up a map and you will try to locate gold through the use of the map. If you convey the idea with complete clarity and point out the advantages to the sub-conscious, then you will be able to detect gold *if there is any there.*

'Then a question about the coming World Leader; will his life be made as miserable and horrible as yours? Will humanity listen to him or will they again just scoff, laugh, demand proof, and scream their nasty heads off? Will he be born in a country that is "politically acceptable" to the rest of the world or will he have to suffer from discrimination too?'

I will tell you this; that World Leader is not any of those over-publicized young people who are screaming around with much press publicity that they and they only can save the world. No, the real World Leader is living privately as yet unknown to the world. When the time comes, and then only, will he move into the limelight of unwanted publicity.

Yes, he will have suffering, he will have misery, he will be disbelieved, he will be pilloried and persecuted by the Press, but—if his message gets over to even a thousand people he will not have been here in vain. At present there is such a person on this earth. The body is being developed. At the appropriate time transmigration will take place and a greater Entity will come down and carry on from that point. You get something the same in surgery or in art. You get a lesser skilled man to make the opening incision (sorry, no pun intended!), and then when the basic work has been done the Master will take over and do that for which he has been acclaimed as a Master. After the Master has done the successful operation, some lesser surgeon, for instance, will 'stitch up' and generally clean up the mess. It is the same thing with the Leaders of the World who come here and take over a body which is already trained to operate on the Earth. It would be such a waste if a great Entity had to spend about thirty years kicking about on this crummy old Earth of ours. That is why such people take over by transmigration.

I have some questions here from a gentleman whose name is famous in connection with tea bags! He wants to know about longevity. He asks: 'Some people are under the impression that due to modern medical science it is possible to live longer at the present time than, say, two hundred years ago. Is the answer no, we can just get a maximum life span and it cannot be exceeded, but if we are foolish enough it can be terminated prematurely? Could those early deaths in olden days be due to poverty and improper living conditions, etc.?'

Well now, actually in theory there is no limit to how long a person can live because it all depends upon the memory stored within our brain cells, the memory which enables the body to reproduce identical parts. If we had a good enough memory, and a sub-conscious memory it is, a person could go on living almost indefinitely. Unfortunately at the present stage of evolution the memory decays. It is like the old army story.

There was a long line of men, a hundred men in a row. An officer at one end of the line whispered a message to the man nearest him and told him to whisper it to the next man, and so on. And then the last man produced a message which had little bearing on the original subject.

We get the same thing with humans. We can say that a patch of skin has worn out and the body-entity wants a repair job done, but the memory is a bit sick of all these repetitions so there is a slight divergence in the type, texture, or colour of the skin. So the person might get one of those brown patches which are a symptom of increasing age, or a fastidious lady may get too much skin and find she's got a nasty wrinkle, and so she spreads a lot of goo on her face to try to shrink the skin.

Eventually there will come a time when people can live five or six hundred years, and it will come about not through anything special in the way of surgery or medicine, but through a development in electro-chemistry because if we could get our chemical balance right we could get our brain voltages correct, and in that case cancer, schizophrenia, and other things would be cured. For example, a person gets over-tired with too much work so his body chemistry is depleted of those chemicals which build up the necessary voltages to keep him in operating condition. Now if the person suddenly takes in some sugar, for example, (provided he is not diabetic!) he gets a sudden spurt of energy and the tiredness goes away for a time. In other words, his battery has been recharged and he functions again on the normal level.

My old friend, Jim Dodd, who lives in America, has just sent me a copy of a newspaper cutting about 'electrical medicine', and Jim Dodd is highly interested in my comments because he has had a knock on the noggin through a car accident and from what I can gather from his letter the surgeons just about filleted him—but kept only the bones! An unfortunate state for a person to be in. Now, presumably, if he walks down the street the dogs come after him to take a chew at the bones. But there it is; it makes one think isn't life wonderful!

But this cutting about electrical medicine is only the stuff I have been telling you about before saying, 'We seldom stop to think that our bodies run on electricity, but they do.' And Jim Dodd wants to know if there is any truth in what the author of this article writes. The answer is—yes, there is a lot of truth in it, but the sad thing about the whole affair is that medicine generally is at least a hundred years behind the times. Orthodox doctors dare not risk their reputation in even attempting anything which has not been approved after ten years use by some of the trade unions controlling doctors.

Oh yes, let's bear in mind constantly that doctors have trade unions even more powerful than the teamsters unions, and they are kept rigidly in line. Some of the medical members of the doctors' unions have nothing on Jimmy Hoffa for discipline! But that is taking us away from this stuff sent by Jim Dodd.

Yes, one can do a tremendous amount with electricity. Electricity, properly applied, can speed healing, can the more easily unite broken bones. At one end of the scale there is electrocution when a fellow is literally knocked out of his body and his astral goes wandering off. At the other end of the scale people could even be helped to get born by electricity.

Jim Dodd is particularly interested in electrical anaesthesia, and the article which he sends seems to be very much out of date, or, like a fat woman seen from the back, all behind, because electrical anaesthesia is a definite proven thing. Two electrodes are placed beside the head and a mild current is switched on, a DC current, and the patient or victim goes

160

dreamlessly to sleep because the astral says, in effect, 'Gee, I don't like this; it's too hot for my feet. I'm going!' And so the astral gets out of the body in a hurry and doesn't return until the current is switched off.

Actually, if a person knew how he could put anyone to sleep without any difficulty at all, that is one of the dangers because now—well, we all know the old story of the white slavers with their chloroform pad. They swipe someone across the face with a cloth soaked in chloroform and the poor innocent defenceless girl goes to sleep instantly, but that is not so, you know. It takes a long time to put a person to sleep by that method. It is easier to use a coal hammer.

Hey though, don't go trying tricks with electricity (or coal hammers!) because it is very very wrong indeed to commit suicide, just as wrong as it is to commit murder. So when you read these electrical details don't get crazy bees in your bonnet because—I repeat—*suicide is a very bad thing indeed to do.*

But if a person knows the very simple technique of electro-anaesthesia, just about anyone could be taken unawares and put to sleep. Possibly that is why doctors are so cautious about it, they probably want to have some rigmarole or ritual so that it appears to be more difficult than it is. What can be done is this; a patient—let's imagine this, shall we?—is wheeled into the operating room annexe. The anaesthetist just puts two little electrodes at carefully determined spots on each side of the head. The current is switched on and the patient is asleep as quickly as switching off a light, no gasping, nothing of that kind at all—the patient is 'switched off when the current is switched on'.

Then, with the operation finished, the current is switched off and the patient awakens instantly without any recollection of pain or anything else to do with the operation, and, interestingly enough, the painlessness effect lasts from twelve to twenty hours during which time the patient is fully conscious and sweetly reasonable, that is, of course, if he was sweetly reasonable before. But this form of anaesthetic will come into use eventually. It is just a matter of breaking down the bonds of prejudice and unadulterated fright. It is too much like electrocution, isn't it, to lie down and have someone put electrodes on your head and then switch on the current and—bonk, you are out!

Electric induction of anaesthesia is a great blessing in operations to the liver, the kidneys, etc. In kidney operations it is necessary to have a terrific amount of chemical or gaseous (same thing) anaesthetic, but the poor wretched kidneys which are being operated upon have to suffer the operation and also have the task of eliminating the chemicals used in the anaesthetic, and that makes it very, very difficult. Further, getting such a load of noxious chemicals in one's system can upset one's metabolism no matter what the operation should be, whereas in electrical induction there are no chemicals of any kind because—going back to our radio days—when the electric current flows through certain conduits of the brain it just acts in the same way as the grid bias battery of the old radio receivers one used so many years ago. It set up a back pressure of current which prevented the flow of brain-electricity which meant that a person was conscious. And that is all there is to it. No pain, no suffering, no drugs, no chemicals, only sound sleep without any after-effects.

So there you are, friend Jim Dodd. When you read this you will have your answer. It's a pity you couldn't have had this stuff when you had your operations, eh?

Let us continue with some of our questions and answers which seem to interest an astonishingly large number of people. So here is a question about exorcism. The question is: 'A number of men of the Cloth claim to have performed this operation, some with great success. Others admit to poor results. Now, if they are not fully clairvoyant, *and they are not*, how will they know who or what they are dealing with? Is it permissible to state what actually takes place?'

Yes, it is. If a place is being haunted then it means that there is some undesirable entity present. The entity emanates an unpleasant thought form or thought pattern. People become aware of the presence of such an entity without being able to say how they are aware. In some cases they can see the entity. In other cases they can feel the entity, but when they are completely non-clairvoyant the person who is being haunted gets a great feeling of unease, strange impressions cross his mind,

162

and even the least clairvoyant *knows* that there is something wrong.

Those who can do exorcism are people with a strong thought-wave, that is, they can project the thought of something very strongly. Now, a clergyman who has got himself thoroughly hypnotized in the belief that he is doing something as the Lord's right hand, and sometimes the left hand as well, gets his thought-wave boosted up because of his self-induced hypnotism. He thinks he is the answer to the maiden's prayer, or possibly the answer to the Lord's prayer would be more suitable. But he is so sure of himself that he turns all the knobs on full in his thought processes, and the entity who is doing the haunting doesn't like it a bit. He thinks, in effect, 'Oh good gracious me, I can't stick this fellow. If he's going to hang around like this—I'm off.' And so the haunting force takes off for pastures new where there are no clergymen who are going to project unpleasant thoughts. And that is all there is to that. It is just a matter of telepathy because no matter what anyone believes, every person is telepathic to a certain extent. It has been proved, for instance, that even when a non-telepath (self-proclaimed) was put to a test, when he thought at a non-telepathic victim he could influence the pulse and the blood pressure of his test subject. That has actually been proved. Quite a lot of things have been proved about clairvoyance and telepathy, but they have not been made public because gory murders are much better selling attractions.

Here is a touch of humour. It is a paragraph from a letter to me. It is headed 'E.S.P.—A Further Illustration to the Accuracy of Your Writings is This. A woman writes in our newspaper to say that she cannot get a night's sleep if the sheets or pillowcases have stripes on them. She can feel the stripes. It doesn't matter if the light is on or not, she doesn't have to see those stripes to know that they are there, and they disturb her sleep.' Oh yes, that was a quotation, apparently, from some English newspaper, I wish I knew which newspaper it was.

Here is a question which could be interesting. The question is: 'Would you explain the destiny of the evolution of the plant and animal kingdoms?'

A lot of people believe that plants evolve into animals, and

163

animals evolve into humans, but that is not so. You have never heard of a horse turning into a cow, have you, and you have never heard of a lettuce leaf turning into a bird. The animal kingdom, the human kingdom, and the vegetable kingdom are things completely apart, things completely different, and I am telling you in all seriousness—this is not a joke by any means, it is the absolute truth—on certain other planets animals take the place of humans. On other planets the vegetable kingdom reigns supreme. For example, there is a planet where plants such as trees are able to manage a slow mode of locomotion. They pick up their modified roots and move to a different location, and sink their roots down again that they may absorb the necessary nourishment. So the evolution is this; a cabbage may not be very conscious on this Earth from the human standpoint, but even so cabbages can recognize people and they can recognize emotions. Oh, you don't believe that? Well, that has already been proved, that has been proved in laboratory tests. So that if your Auntie Macassar was a happy old soul her aspidistra would be happy too and would grow better and have a better colour. While the plant of Melissa Mugwump, a sour old biddy, would also be affected and would have poor colour and stunted growth. The moral in this seems to be smile sweetly on your potatoes and they will grow better for you!

Evolution is ever upwards, so the vegetables and plants with which we are today acquainted on this Earth will in time become sentient highly intelligent persons of the plant world in a different evolution, in a different incarnation. Animals also grow upwards in spiritual stature. It doesn't mean to say that your pet cat is suddenly going to start out and paint pictures better than Rembrandt or suddenly start making radios on the kitchen table. No, their values are quite different. Their values consist of spiritual attainment just as in the old days before the advent of Communism and the television and Press, in the Far Far East only things of the spirit mattered, things of purity, things of true religious thought. People earned enough money to keep them alive so that they could progress through this Earth and not have to come back to it. Humans, then, in the far off days, were better people than the humans of today because nowadays humans are contaminated with TV, contaminated with the Press, and contaminated with too many commercial interests. It doesn't matter nowadays in the West how good living a person is, all that matters is—how big is his bank account. In that latter reading I don't amount to anything at all! But I do know quite a few things about the spirit and a person cannot take his bank account with him to the Other Side. My 'bank account' is knowledge, knowledge which I can take with me when I go.

Curiously enough I have just got another question about that: 'Have minerals on any planets got intelligence?'

And the answer is a definite Yes. Now, I have already told you that on certain other planets the carbon molecule is not the building brick of that system, it may be a silicate, and there are 'stones' of silicate composition who are actually thinking, moving entities. If you could go there and see them (you can't so don't bother your travel agent) you would have to stay a whole lifetime before you saw even a twitch of movement because if a creature can live for a million or two years, then speed of locomotion doesn't matter greatly. So moving stones take their time. They are about as slow as the people I had to move my stuff quite recently.

Hey, do you know something? Now that I thought I had finished dealing with transmigration another question comes up. Here it is: 'It is said the body changes molecule for molecule every seven years. What actually happens? Certain Eastern books which give this information could be distorted in translation. This is for those who doubt changing of bodies.'

Well, let us give an imaginary case, shall we? Little Billy Smith can't get on with life, everything goes wrong for him and he is sick and tired of living on Earth where everyone seems to 'be on his back'. He contemplates suicide which surely is a stupid thing to do because if he commits suicide he will be slapped back to Earth in a worse condition. But anyway, before he does knock himself off he gets a message during his sleep. Tom Thomas, who is in the astral, wants to come back to Earth to do a special job, and Tom Thomas has arranged with a special Council who control such things that Billy Smith can part from his body provided he allows Tom

Thomas to take over. So Billy Smith doesn't think much, at first, of somebody else taking over his messy clay body, but as the days go by the more he thinks about it the more ready he becomes to agree. So a deal is made. Billy Smith lies down somewhere, the Silver Cord is parted, but before it can be completely severed it is connected to a Silver Cord sprouted by Tom Thomas, and Tom Thomas, a gentleman of the astral, then enters the body of Billy Smith.

Poor Tom shudders in dismay almost as soon as he gets there. The body is inefficient. The muscles are flabby. The feet don't seem to go where they are directed, and the eyes don't focus very well. In addition, there is a really awful stench from the body. Never mind, Tom will get used to it in time, but he will find that the body isn't too satisfactory, he will be like a pilot in an aeroplane, a pilot who has flown aircraft before but not this particular model. The pilot sits there jittering with fright while he looks at all the different dials and knobs, etc., and then gingerly he puts out his hand to get the machine working. Soon he is able to control the body, but there is always this terrible feeling that one is in an alien body, and that becomes intolerable. So the molecules of that borrowed body, that taken-over body, are changed molecule by molecule, so that at the end of seven years the body of Billy Smith is no longer of the same composition, everything has been changed, and now there is the body of Tom Thomas. And Tom Thomas is happy again—more or less—because he has the body to which he is accustomed.

In the days of long ago high priests were able to teach people how to do these things. It was much like going to a car showroom and having the head salesman there demonstrate new models. Bodies could be tried out to see which one was most suitable, and as I have said previously, in Atlantis and Lemuria special 'no ownership' bodies were kept available for travelling Gardeners of the Earth. The bodies were used in much the same way as one rents a car, goes on a journey, and returns the car.

A question here is: 'Yetis; many claim to have seen them and photographed them in various parts of the world. Is this correct? Are the heads, hands, etc. on show in certain places just manufactured objects to attract visitors?'

It is a strange thought, isn't it, people have gone to the Moon, robot ships have gone to Mars, and other robot ships are going to other worlds, yet Man has not yet thoroughly explored nor investigated all aspects of this world. There are many parts of the Earth, in Canada, for instance, and Alaska, Tibet, India, and Africa where humans have never been, and in those remote areas there are remnants of a race which should have expired centuries before. Yes, there are 'yetis'. These people are the last dregs of a race which has left the Earth except for them. Think of people trying to drain a lake of fish; for some reason the people owning the lake want all the fish out so it can be restocked with a different type. They use nets and all sorts of other devices to catch the fish and transport them elsewhere, and then the lake is restocked with a different species of fish. But from time to time there are reports of one or two fish of the original type who have briefly been seen but not caught. You can't catch everything. A fish may be a pregnant fish (a twerp, I believe the correct term is), it may be hidden in a small hole in a rock and so escape the nets, and when that fish shoots out her eggs or whatever she does, and the eggs hatch then more fish are born. We get the same thing here on Earth in the remotest areas. But it's a good thing they are in remote areas because there are so many bloodthirsty people who want to go out and shoot themselves a yeti so they can have his skin in front of the fireplace or something.

As for many of the 'specimens'—well, you can go to a wax work museum and you can see some remarkable 'people' there, but they are only wax figures, aren't they? I shouldn't believe too strongly in the claims that here at last is the body of a yeti.

Question: 'What are the Pyramids? Where did they originate? How were they built? What is the real use of them? And will a pyramid shaped object preserve things?'

That is meant to be a question! It seems like a whole load of questions to me, but let us see what we can do about it.

Pyramids are nothing but marker beacons. If you live near the sea or a river which is used by ships you will see buoys in the water. If you live near an airport you will see marker beacons to guide aircraft. A pyramid is that shape because that is the most enduring shape and because it has four sides which can help reflect a signal.

In the days when the Gardeners of the Earth came to this world they came in space ships and the space ships had to be guided in just the same way as a ship entering port has to be guided by the colouration and configuration of objects anchored in the water.

When these pyramids were built there were many other devices on the Earth which now have been lost to Man, devices, for example, which could nullify the effects of gravity. Then one could put a sort of clamp on a huge block of stone and turn a switch and adjust a knob, and the block would rise up into the air and it could be guided to its destination.

This is not fiction. This is fact. Let me tell you something; in the U.S.A. a special hotel was built. It was built first as a framework with a lot of pigeon holes, and then a powerful motor was fixed on the top of special boxes, each box was a completely equipped room, and the motor was started and rotor blades lifted the box up to the right height when it could be slid into one of these pigeon holes. I saw this in, I think, 'Practical Mechanics' not too long ago. I wished I could have produced the picture for you. It was interesting.

So the pyramids were built by anti-gravity machines.

The Sphinx? You ask about that also. The Sphinx is a special marker device marking the location of a great horde of 'treasure' hidden beneath, the treasure in this case is a museum of the arts and sciences of a long-bygone age. That is the purpose of the Sphinx.

Oh, in case you didn't know, there are quite a few pyramids throughout the world. Egypt does not have a monopoly of pyramids. There have been pyramids in Mexico and in Brazil, in certain parts of China, and in various other locations, and, I repeat, they were just marker beacons. Space ships could 'home' on the signals emitted from these pyramids and then come in to the desired spaceport. That, I repeat most solemnly, is the absolute truth; it is not fiction.

Here is a question which will interest many of you. The question is: 'Where is the lower astral? What is it?'

168

The lower astral is a place, or zone, or time continuum where the vibrations are two-dimensional instead of three, where conditions are not harmonious. It is an astral zone where thought is not clear, where it is not possible to create artistically. It is what one might term a twilight zone, and just think of this; you are looking at a picture in the dusk and you cannot see the colours, can you? You may be able to determine the subject of the picture, but the dusk stops the colours and you may see instead a more or less uniform set of greyish tones. You have to have daylight in order to see colours. In the same way, if one goes to the astral above this Earth one can see colours which are not visible on this Earth, but if one goes to the lower astral, that is, if one is caught in this mesh of lower vibrations one cannot even see the tawdry colours which one can see upon this Earth.

CHAPTER TEN

'Aw, lookit de owd guy wid de wheels!' shrieked the Young Gentleman in the shopping centre. 'Gee!' breathed his sleazy companion, 'Well, ain't that sharp?' Eyes darted right and left, gawking at any passing thing that caught their vapid attention, the two young men slouched off.

In the near distance a slow-moving figure reluctantly detached himself from the self-imposed task of supporting a concrete pillar. Chewing hard, he lurched over and, with the skill of long practise, parked a wad of well-chewed gum on the side window of the nearest store.

Hands hooked in his belt, he stood wide-legged and still chewed from long habit. 'Sa-ay,' he uttered eventually, 'that shore is a mighty fine rig you got there. Steer it with your feet?' Not waiting for an answer, he deftly retrieved his parked gum, shoved it back in his mouth, and wearily meandered off.

'Omigawd, lookat *that*!' yelled a fat woman with inches of slip showing beneath her skirt. 'Yaas, *wonderful* what they get up to, ain't it?' bellowed her companion.

The old man in the wheelchair snorted with disgust. An elderly lady standing in front gave a sudden start with fright at the sound. Just then there was a sudden lurch and groceries cascaded all around. 'Yer wuz gwain too fast!' shrilled a tattered woman. 'Didn see ya at all I didn, yer wuz gwain too fast.'

The old man, whose wheelchair had been quite stationary, moved off. 'Ahh!' he muttered to himself. 'Let me get going and finish the book. Then perhaps we can look for a saner place than British Columbia.'

Another old man was dying. Lying on his bed in the dark-

170

ened room he watched with fast diminishing sight the gleam of light high up where the curtains did not completely obscure sunlight. A shaft of light struck across the room and made just a splotch on the dingy paint.

The old man stirred restlessly, almost mindlessly. He was in no pain. Instead there was a sensation of cold creeping upwards from his feet to his knees, higher.

Dully he wondered when the angels would gather about him. He had been an ardent believer in his religion all his life. He believed in angels, he believed that at his passing he would go to the Pearly Gates, he believed——

The light faded as if a cloud had passed across the face of the sun, but simultaneously a greater Light came on. The old man was now feeling the cold, the cold as of ice, creeping upwards past his hips, up to his waist. Slowly—slowly—it reached up towards his heart.

Like a sunburst light enveloped the room. He gazed about him with eyes which were fast going blind, shadowy figures were about him, figures with wings. There was the rustling of voices, not understandable to him yet because he was seeing as through a filmy gauze veil.

The cold crept up and struck at his heart. With a last convulsive gasp the old man started finally to die as his heart stopped and his lungs ceased to pulse. Now conditions were speeded up because with the cessation of breathing there was the termination of oxygen to the brain. The physical body twitched in the last nervous reactions, twitched without the old man feeling the twitches, without any pain. He was now beyond pain, beyond feeling in the body.

The blind eyes, now dead eyes, stared upward motionless. Within the body there was the rustling of fluids and the sighing of winds. There was crepitation as joints loosened, as muscles relaxed their tense grip on life.

Slowly a bluish-white mist emerged from the dead body and coalesced into an intangible form over the head. It became more distinct, firmer, in the shape of a nude human, an old old man wracked with suffering. But as it coalesced and became firmer the outlines became smoother, more youthful, more tranquil.

171

Gradually the connecting cord—the Silver Cord—thinned, frayed, and parted. The newly-coalesced astral form hesitated a moment then gradually, with a slight jerk, started into motion, going faster and faster into an unknown plane.

The old man in life had been a close follower of his religion. He hadn't believed in reincarnation. He had believed in the resurrection of the body at the Day of Judgment. He believed that all bodies buried or burned eventually were collected together and clothed again with flesh, even after ten thousand years. Now in the astral form he was lost, lost and wandering, victim to the fallacious beliefs to which he had subscribed for so long. He believed in nothing but the dead resting in their lonely graves or collected in little piles of ashes from the crematoriums, but he was alive, alive in a different shape. About him he saw alternately black fog of nothingness, and then when a little doubt about his religion came into his awareness he saw another facet of his religion—angels. Desperately he fastened on the idea of angels. Reluctantly he threw aside the thought of resurrection—what was resurrection to him?—He was alive, wasn't he, in a different state? But he could see angels, couldn't he, so what was this talk about resurrection? Let him live for the moment, he thought, and then he seemed to drop to the ground. His feet—astral feet? Spirit feet? They felt very solid to him. The ground felt soft and springy and warm to his bare feet. But he dropped to the ground and the veil was drawn aside, he looked about him. Angels were flying through the air, cherubims were sitting on clouds, great choirs were singing with monotonous repetition. Away in the distance he saw golden light. Away in the distance he saw the Pearly Gates.

Swiftly he moved into action, running across the springy turf, inexorably drawing nearer to the Pearly Gates. At last, after an unspecified time, he reached those monumental edifices which towered so high above him. A gleaming figure outside with a flashing sword of golden light barred the way. 'Who are you?' asked a voice.

The old man gave his name. From just inside the Gate another sparkling figure opened a great book and moistening his thumbs with his lips riffled through the pages. 'Ah yes,'

172

said the second voice. 'Yes, we expected you here. Enter!'

The Great Book of Records was closed. The Pearly Gates were opened, and the old man, now a young naked man, entered.

For some time the newly arrived visitor was in a state of ecstasy at the realization of all that his religion had taught him. Angels, cherubims, seraphims. The Heavenly Host singing in multi-layered choirs, St. Peter, the Recording Angel, and the Great Book of all Knowledge wherein was kept the record of every soul upon Earth, in which was recorded the good and the bad of every person who had ever lived.

Gradually, though, the old man—now the newest visitor— began to feel uneasy. There were inconsistencies. This was not real, this was pantomime, this was stage stuff. Where had he gone wrong? Was it something wrong with his religion? Then the thought came to him about resurrection? Well, he thought to himself, is this as ungenuine as resurrection? What about resurrection? How could dead bodies which had long rotted away be reassembled at the last trump of a great bugle? Where would all those people stand, how would they be clothed, how would they be fed? And this angelic host, this glimpse of Heaven—disappointing place, I am beginning to doubt my senses.

No sooner had he said that to himself than there was a great clap as of thunder and the whole edifice fell around him with broken shards of the Pearly Gates and the golden light extinguished. But—*stop!*—a greater light came on. The old man, now a visitor, looked about him in awe. *This* was more like it. Running towards him he saw people whom he had known in his last life on Earth, people he had loved. He saw a beloved pet coming towards him and jumping up at him and shouting with delight.

Another figure came towards him and said, 'Ah, now you are released from your delusions. Now you have reached a true home, the Land of the Golden Light. Here you will sojourn for a while while you and you alone decide what you want to do.'

So it is that many religions lead one astray. So it is that one can read of any religion and learn thereby, but the true wisdom

173

comes in keeping an open mind so that when the time comes for the transition from this life to another you—and you—and you—*everyone* can go to the state for which his or her evolution and attainment have fitted him, for in the Greater Plan of things even those who have passed over have to be protected from their own folly. If a person believes that he will go to an imaginary Heaven, then it will be put on show for him until he sees the flaws.

If a person thinks that he is going to a land of ineffable delights where dancing girls are always there to entertain him, then he will have such things put on for him until he outgrows such transient things.

And if a Womans Lib leader had as her idea of Heaven a place where all men are slaves, then no doubt that also could be produced for her. And such plays can go on until the person concerned eventually comes to see the fallacy of such stage acts, until such time as the person concerned grows up spiritually and mentally and can accept the Land of the Golden Light for what it is, a place of reality, a place different yet not so different as that which they so recently left. A place with the evil purged out, a place where one can only meet those who are compatible, a place where there is no hatred, no enmity, no poverty, and no suffering. A place where one, in full awareness of one's acts, judges one's past endeavours and failings and decides what shall be done in the future.

But the clack of the typewriter must cease. The platen must no longer be twirled, and the papers must not be fed in and pulled out—typed, for the allotted span of this book has come to pass. Now it has to be sent to Respected Agent Knight to pass on to Respected Publisher!

Miss Cleopatra Rampa sighed with relief as she turned to Taddy Rampa: 'Oh, thank goodness!' she said. 'Now he's got rid of this stuff perhaps he'll have time for us.'

It remains then to do only two more tasks. The first is to thank Mrs. Rampa for her constant vigilance in reading the typescript and checking slight errors. And secondly, one must really thank Mrs. Sheelagh Rouse, a loyal companion throughout the years, for the hard work she has done in typing all this for us.

THE END

A SELECTION OF FINE READING
AVAILABLE IN CORGI BOOKS

Novels

General

☐ 552 09332 7	GO ASK ALICE	*Anonymous* 30p
☐ 552 09292 4	LOVE, LIFE AND SEX	*Barbara Cartland* 35p
☐ 552 09185 5	THE FUNDAMENTALS OF SEX (illustrated)	
	Dr. Philip Cauthery & Dr. Martin Cole 50p	
☐ 552 09392 0	THE MYSTERIOUS UNKNOWN (illustrated)	
	Robert Charroux 50p	
☐ 552 09151 0	THE DRAGON AND THE PHOENIX	*Eric Chou* 50p
☐ 552 08800 5	CHARIOTS OF THE GODS? (illustrated)	*Erich von Daniken* 35p
☐ 552 09073 2	RETURN TO THE STARS (illustrated)	*Erich von Daniken* 40p
☐ 552 09331 9	OPERATION RHINO (illustrated)	*John Gordon Davis* 40p
☐ 552 07400 4	MY LIFE AND LOVES	*Frank Harris* 65p
☐ 552 98748 4	MAKING LOVE (Photographs)	*Walter Hartford* 85p
☐ 552 09062 X	THE SENSUOUS MAN	*'M'* 35p
☐ 552 09293 2	GOLF'S WINNING STROKE: PUTTING (illustrated)	
	Tom Michael 50p	
☐ 552 09290 8	INTIMATE BEHAVIOUR	*Desmond Morris* 40p
☐ 552 08010 1	THE NAKED APE	*Desmond Morris* 30p
☐ 552 09232 0	SECRET OF THE ANDES	*Brother Philip* 30p
☐ 552 09390 4	CANDLELIGHT	*T. Lobsang Rampa* 30p
☐ 552 09266 5	ANY WOMAN CAN	*David R. Reuben M.D.* 50p
☐ 552 09044 1	SEX ENERGY	*Robert S. de Ropp* 35p
☐ 552 09250 9	THE MANIPULATED MAN	*Esther Vilar* 35p
☐ 552 09145 6	THE NYMPHO AND OTHER MANIACS	*Irvine Wallace* 40p
☐ 552 09391 2	OMNIVORE	*Dr. Lyall Watson* 30p

Western

☐ 552 09095 6	APACHE	*Will Levington Comfort* 30p
☐ 552 09227 4	YOU'RE IN COMMAND NOW, MR. FOG No. 71	
	J. T. Edson 30p	
☐ 552 09298 3	THE BIG GUN No. 72	*J. T. Edson* 30p
☐ 552 09327 0	SET TEXAS BACK ON HER FEET No. 73	*J. T. Edson* 30p
☐ 552 09191 X	TREASURE MOUNTAIN	*Louis L'Amour* 30p
☐ 552 09264 9	THE FERGUSON RIFLE	*Louis L'Amour* 30p
☐ 552 09387 4	THE MAN FROM SKIBBEREEN	*Louis L'Amour* 30p
☐ 552 09287 8	KILLING FOR THE LAW No. 21	*Louis Masterson* 25p
☐ 552 09328 9	THE BUTCHER FROM GUERRERO No. 22	
	Louis Masterson 25p	
☐ 552 08810 2	SUDDEN—OUTLAWED	*Oliver Strange* 25p
☐ 552 09388 2	HIGH PLAINS DRIFTER	*Ernest Tidyman* 30p

Crime

☐ 552 09384 X	DEATH IN HIGH PLACES	*John Creasey* 30p
☐ 552 09385 8	DEATH IN FLAMES	*John Creasey* 30p
☐ 552 09386 6	THE BARON COMES BACK	*John Creasey* 30p
☐ 552 09310 6	CAGE UNTIL TAME	*Laurence Henderson* 35p
☐ 552 09262 3	THE EXECUTIONER: CHICAGO WIPEOUT	
	Don Pendleton 30p	
☐ 552 09325 4	THE EXECUTIONER: VEGAS VENDETTA	*Don Pendleton* 30p
☐ 552 09326 2	THE EXECUTIONER: CARIBBEAN KILL	*Don Pendleton* 30p
☐ 552 09111 1	THE ERECTION SET	*Mickey Spillane* 40p
☐ 552 09273 8	SHAFT HAS A BALL	*Ernest Tidyman* 30p
☐ 552 09309 2	SHAFT AMONG THE JEWS	*Ernest Tidyman* 35p

All these books are available at your bookshop or newsagent: or can be ordered direct from the publisher. Just tick the titles you want and fill in the form below.

CORGI BOOKS, Cash Sales Department, P.O. Box 11, Falmouth, Cornwall.
Please send cheque or postal order, no currency, and allow 7p per book to cover the cost of postage and packing in the U.K. (5p if more than one copy) 7p per book overseas.

NAME ....

ADDRESS ....

(NOV. 73) ....